Also by Willard H. Porter:
13 Flat

How to Enjoy
the Quarter Horse

Willard H. Porter

South Brunswick and New York: A. S. Barnes and Company
London: Thomas Yoseloff Ltd

© 1973 by A. S. Barnes and Co., Inc.

A. S. Barnes and Co., Inc.
Cranbury, New Jersey 08512

Thomas Yoseloff Ltd
108 New Bond Street
London W1Y OQX, England

Library of Congress Cataloging in Publication Data

Porter, Willard H   1920–
    How to enjoy the quarter horse.

    1. Quarter horse. I. Title. _1. Horses_
SF293.Q3P67   1973   636.1'08'   72-5173
ISBN 0-498-01215-8

All photographs are by Willard H. Porter, unless otherwise credited.

Printed in the United States of America

To
Renée and Van Smelker,
who love Quarter Horses—
especially
the boot-scoot-hustle-and-hoot kind

Contents

Acknowledgments

My credentials for writing this book may not be appropriate under the heading of "Acknowledgments." But please know that while I was editor of the *Quarter Horse Journal,* from 1949 through 1953, and publisher of *Hoofs and Horns,* from 1957 through 1966, I met hundreds and hundreds of people—far too many to thank here—who helped immeasurably with much of the material in this volume that relates to the Quarter Horse.

Just a handful of these people to whom I am particularly indebted includes Raymond Hollingsworth, Katy Peake, Punk Snyder, Ronald Mason, King Merritt, Tom Fuller, Chuck King, Peter Hurd, Roy Davis, Don Flint, Ray Lewis, Roy Parks, Kemper Chafin, Olga and Jess Hankins, Fred and Kate Lowry, Jess Goodspeed, Roy Wales, Don Dodge, Bob Sutherland, Casey and Fred Darnell, Marion Flynt, Ralph Morrison, Dick Spencer III, Alvie Cole, C. L. Maddon, Melville Haskell, Ike Rude, Walt Wardlaw, Art Pollard, Johnnie Burson, Nancy Binford, Jack Clifford, Tom Finley, Bob Denhardt, Troy Fort, Elmer Hepler, Toots Mansfield, Bob Moore, Boozer Page, Dink Parker, Chuck Sheppard, Rukin Jelks, Geech Partin, B. J. Pierce, Buddy Reger, Bud Warren, Jake Meyer, Roy Gill, Max Schott, Jimmy Culwell, Walt Coburn, Zack Wood, Jr., Jimmie Randals, and many others. (Statistical material appears through the courtesy of the American Quarter Horse Association.)

The author also wants to thank the following publications for permission to reprint (in slightly altered form) some of the material found on these pages: the *Western Horseman,* the *Cattleman, Western Livestock Journal,* the *Quarter Horse Journal,* and *Horseman: The Magazine of Western Riding.*

Thanks also to the photographers whose work appears in this volume. And a tip of the hat to the American Quarter Horse Association, whose warm cooperation is appreciated and whose tremendous growth in three decades (plus) points up the great popularity of the Quarter Horse.

And, finally, a word of thanks to the equine about which I am writing. If he were not something special, well, I suppose there just would not be any book called *How to Enjoy the Quarter Horse.*

Introduction

There are two good reasons why I decided on the title, *How to Enjoy the Quarter Horse:* a rider can do more things—and do them well—on a Quarter Horse than he can on any other equine breed, and a rider can have more fun on a Quarter Horse than he can on any other equine breed. And, of course, that goes for your daughter, wife, and mother-in-law, too.

I do not want to sound like a press agent, but it is hard not to. For, you see, an awful lot of hullabaloo has been kicked up over the Quarter Horse—and, give or take a few preposterous statements, it is all true.

I do draw the line at the following classified advertisement, for instance, which appeared some years ago in the *Ellensburg Daily Record,* Ellensburg, Washington:

FOR SALE: 4-year-old appaloosa gelding. Should make good quarter horse.

In the history of domestic livestock, few—if any—animals have created such a sensation as has America's most popular equine breed. Horses and cattle, goats and pigs, have usually been named for the geographical localities in which they originated. Not so the Quarter Horse. He was named for a measure of distance—440 yards or a quarter of a mile.

This strange nomenclature was tacked onto the horse over three hundred years ago, when he used to sprint this distance in the infant, racing-minded United States colonies of Maryland, Virginia, and the Carolinas. Yet up until a few years ago, most horsemen did not know this. The derivation of his name was usually shrugged off with, "Oh, he's three-quarters horse and one-quarter confusion."

Even today, with more people using, riding, and enjoying Quarter Horses than any other four-legged mode of transportation, you cannot find many people who will exactly agree what this horse is, where he comes from, or what he is supposed to do. I have been connected in one way or another with the breed since 1935 and I have heard an awful lot of muttering in answer to the question: "What is a Quarter Horse?"

The truth is, nobody can give a simple definition of these horses. For the horses are not that simple. They are puzzles, enigmas, and paradoxes, yet they are the best loved horseflesh in the world.

One of the zaniest but, perhaps, most accurate definitions I have ever heard was the answer that the veteran cowboy gave to the neophyte owner. When the newcomer asked, "What is a Quarter Horse?" the old-timer said, "Shucks, that's easy . . . a Quarter Horse is what one fellow will tell another it ain't."

Gene Nichols, a Flagler, Colorado, rancher, once said: "To me a true Quarter Horse is one that can run a quarter of a mile or any part thereof faster than any other . . . and is of whatever bloodlines necessary to produce this early foot."

Sparks Rust of Del Rio, Texas, said: "A Quarter Horse is a cowboy's horse that can do it all."

And Rex C. Cauble, a Denton, Texas, rancher, waxing eloquently over his favorite mount, said: "He's half a ton of poised and controlled energy, held on an easy rein and a hair trigger. He's a workin' man who can earn his keep on the range all week—and be a handsome dandy at the track on Sunday afternoon. He's proud when he stands; looks lazy when he walks. But when he runs he can whip the tears from the corner of your eyes and plaster your hat brim against the crown. He's big in the haunches, supple in the withers, stout in the neck and wide across the chest . . . to hold his great heart. He's thunder and lightning between your knees and a poem in flight across the pasture. He's cow-smart and brave—though sometimes a clown— and to the man with sky in his eye and mud on his boot, the Quarter Horse is a faithful hand . . . and a friend."

With supporters like this, what horse needs a public relations man? No horse, really! But the Quarter Horse has got one, anyhow, in the sponsoring organization, the American Quarter Horse Association, which has registered over three quarters of a million of these horses since the first AQHA *Stud Book* was opened in 1941.

Here is how the AQHA public relations department looks at the animal for which it was founded: "In an era that has spawned history's most massive program of horsemanship strictly for pleasure and sport, the Quarter Horse serves a multitude of interests. From cow camp to roundup, in national cutting contests and rodeos, at race meets, for trail rides and on the show circuit, this versatile animal continues to gather supporters from every walk of life. He can do more things better than any horse that ever stood outdoors."

At the end of 1971, 772,641 horses had been registered, with 16,510 of this figure being in foreign countries. There were close to 100,000 horses registered during 1971 by the association. There were a quarter of a million entries in 1971 at the 1,480 AQHA-sanctioned horse shows for adults in the United States and Canada, in addition to the 132,118 entries in the 1,361 approved shows for boys and girls.

There are more shows annually for Quarter Horses than there are for all other breeds of horses combined.

Significant proof of the Quarter Horse industry's sound economic base is evidenced by 111,007 transfers of ownership recorded in 1971, up six percent over the previous year, which simply means that breeders and owners who want to sell their horses are assured of a strong market.

In addition to short-distance racing, where the really big money is, the biggest boom today in the industry is being stimulated by juniors. And the AQHA, recognizing the value of youthful participation, was the first equine registry to establish a program whereby youngsters eighteen years of age and under may compete at sanctioned shows apart from adults for handsome trophies. The American Junior Quarter Horse Association was formed in 1970, and the first annual AJQHA convention was also held then in Amarillo, Texas, home of the AQHA, when a full slate of junior officers was elected to head up the new organization.

But the parents—the dads and the moms—are still the bosses who run the gigantic association, operating it through directors elected by the group's members. The directors, in turn, elect the officers.

There have been some administrative storms in the past and there are bound to be some storms in the future, if for no other reason than the fact that horsemen and horsewomen are characteristically strong-willed and opinionated. And there are lots of opinions, as we have indicated, concerning this horse.

So let's take an in-depth look at the Quarter Horse. Let's read on to see what you can do with him and how you can enjoy him.

Willard H. Porter

Tucson, Arizona

How to Enjoy
the Quarter Horse

1
What Is a Quarter Horse?

"The American Quarter Horse is not only an established breed of remote origin, but he is the most useful type for nearly all western ranch purposes." These are the words of the late William (Billy) Anson, a Texas stockman originally from England, who was one of the first men to make a study of the Quarter Horse. They were written in 1910.

In those days most Texas ranchers were not as curious as Anson. They cared little about bloodlines and pedigrees. If a horse could do the job for them, that was all that counted. And it was not until thirty years later, at Fort Worth, Texas, that sufficient interest was shown in the Quarter Horse to establish a breed association. Here, in 1940, a group of western horsemen got together and formed the American Quarter Horse Association, dedicated to the revitalization of a breed of horse that, according to historians, was well known in this country almost one hundred years before the first importations of real Thoroughbreds.

The Quarter Horse was America's first genuine breed. His tough fiber enabled him to work six days a week and race on Sundays. He was the first racehorse in the early-day colonies.

For practical reasons, tracks in those times were short, rarely stretching farther than a quarter mile, which was the favorite racing distance before the advent of longer, circular tracks. The breed was not named, as indicated in the Introduction, from any fraction of equine mating, but rather from this short, straightaway distance.

These sprinting courses were often chopped out of the forests on the spur of the moment, or were laid out down the freeway of a village street. Because the courses were neither long nor broad,

In Colonial times the Quarter Horse was a mount that could run a quarter of a mile or less faster than anything else around. Here, Bunny's Bar Maid, sprinting at Ruidoso Downs, shows why.

matched races, usually between two horses, were the rule of the day.

The early races were colorful affairs. Landed gentry rubbed elbows with explorers, trappers, and privateers. The American Indian, decked out in his gaudy headdress, stood at the finish line with the parson and the cavalier. Interest ran high and wagering was feverish. A pair of horses thundered down dusty lanes and in a few seconds it was all over. By 1630, when Governor Nicholson legalized horse racing in Virginia, most of the colonists were enjoying these popular speedsters.

A mixture of Spanish and English equine blood went into the makeup of this relatively small horse with the well-muscled body and the terrific burst of early speed. Spanish horses were first landed in what is now Florida in 1565. The first Virginia importations of English stock occurred in the early 1600s. By the end of the seventeenth century these fleet running horses were considered a breed, or at least a well-defined type.

Later on, with the importation of English stallions of Barb, Arabian, and Galloway blood (the forerunners of the English Thoroughbred), short racing died out in the colonies as longer racing distances came into vogue. But a few people still enjoyed "runnin' 'em short," and the

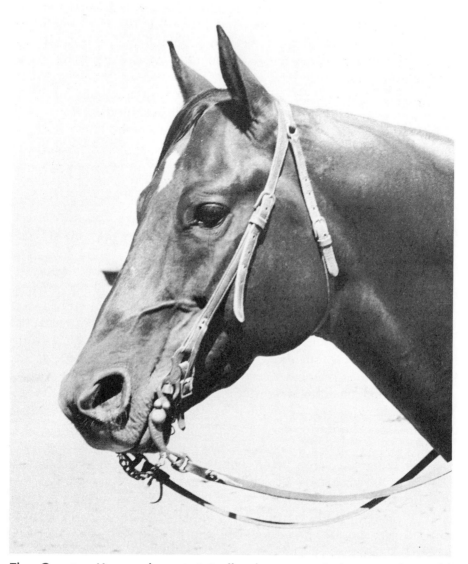

The Quarter Horse, characteristically, has one of the most beautiful, intelligent heads of all equines.

new stallion blood served a double purpose: it upgraded both the long and short racehorse stock.

One of the finest importations was Janus, foaled in 1746 and shipped to Virginia in 1752. A grandson of the Godolphin Barb, he was a spectacular-looking stud, possessing more brawn and ruggedness of conformation than many of his contemporaries. He was bred to an immense number of mares, both Thoroughbred and Quarter Horse type. Of all the imported horses, he alone is considered to have had the greatest influence on most of the "Celebrated" or "Famous American Quarter Running Horses," as they were so identified in P. N. Edgar's *American Race-Turf Register*, published in 1833.

After short racing was eclipsed by long racing, the Quarter Horse moved westward with the frontier. By then the original Spanish blood of the Quarter Horse had been much diluted by infusions of Oriental blood, and the same English blood that went into the formation of the American Thoroughbred. But when the Quarter Horse was bred to the western mustang (feral horses sprung from early Spanish stock), a hybrid vigor developed that, for pure hardiness, has never been equaled.

Actually this cross-breeding of the eastern seaboard sprinter and the mustang tended to downgrade the quality of the resulting progeny even though it did increase its toughness. So still later, in order to get size and still more speed, the Quarter Horse was bred to just about everything in experimental tests. He was bred to the draft horse as well as to the Thoroughbred Remount stud, until by 1940, at the inception of the American Quarter Horse Association, there was an amazing conglomeration of western horse types. And to make matters worse, each owner was justifiably claiming that his horse had the true Quarter Horse heritage.

Although mentioned in the early stud books and turf registeries, the Quarter Horse had never before boasted a formal breed association to champion its cause and to collect, preserve and register past and current breeding efforts. The early life of the AQHA was turbulent. There were as many different viewpoints on the Quarter Horse as there were types within the breed, and the men who started the association soon were the targets of critical fire.

Strangely, the emphasis in 1940 was placed on appearance. And men who had for years used horses—either racing them or working them on ranches—were outraged by the fact that "fat chubs" were winning the halter classes. "This is all wrong," they said, "since the history of the breed has been one of action, speed and performance. No matter how beautiful a horse may be to look at, he's worthless if he can't perform."

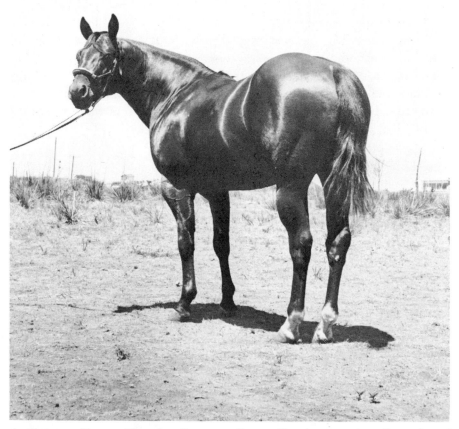

A Quarter Horse, like the Texas stallion, Claude, stands collected with all four feet squared away beneath his solid, muscular body.

So two other associations were organized, the National Quarter Horse Breeders' Association in southern Texas and the American Quarter Racing Association at Tucson, Arizona. And the rift between breeders of varying opinions widened.

In 1949, due to the efforts of intelligent and unhysterical horsemen, who foresaw that a divided association would soon bring chaos to national Quarter Horse competition, the three associations amalgamated into one strong group, today called the American Quarter Horse Association, which stresses conformation, performance, and bloodlines.

There is still an honest difference of opinion between the advocates of the halter type, the ranch type, and the racing type. I believe there always will be. But Quarter Horses are versatile, all-around campaigners. They are the best ranch horses and show horses and the world's fastest short-distance racehorses. They are also personable. They have a gentle disposition; they are tractable and good looking; they are well-rounded performers. They will probably be around for a long time in the future just as they have been, in one way or another, for a long time in the past.

The famous Arizona Quarter Horse stallion, Roper, grazes in a pasture near his Paulden ranch headquarters.

2
Put a Rider in the Saddle

Study of the prehistoric horse does not present much of value from the viewpoint of horse use. The ancestors of what we now call the horse have been given these fancy monikers: *Eohippus, Mesohippus, Parahippus,* and *Mercyhippus.* They were not ridden because they were too small and there was nobody around to ride them anyway.

But ever since the recorded history of the horse, from about 2500 B.C., we know that is was a very important *use* animal. It was used for wars, transportation, migration, and recreation and sport. Polo was played in Persia in 600 B.C., and there has been racing in England since the tenth century.

The *Encyclopaedia Britannica* describes very elegantly what the horse has meant to civilized people: "According to western European mythology and folklore, all the great early civilizations arose among horse-owning, horse-breeding, and horse-using nations; those in which the horse was either unknown or in the feral, or untamed, state were backward, and no great forward movement of mankind was made without the assistance of the horse. So consistently was this the case that the glorified figure of 'the man on horseback' became the symbol of power."

Today, of course, with horse cavalry a thing of the past in major countries, "the man on horseback" is no longer a symbol of power but rather a symbol of perfection—the perfection of man's skill while riding and doing something interesting or pleasing on a horse. The physical body of a man on the physical conformation of a horse produces a wonderful combination. Each complements the other. Man can do so many things on a horse!

The horse on which he does these things with the most proficiency

Youngsters and veterans alike enjoy riding Quarter Horses. Here old-timer Harry Knight of Yuma, Arizona, ropes in a corral from Old Buck.

is the Quarter Horse. Why? Because the Quarter Horse is the best all-around equine athlete in the world. And they are ridden by horsemen of the Americas, the best all-around horsemen in the world. A friend of mine, Tom Fuller, owner of Willow Brook Farms at Catasauqua, Pennsylvania, agrees with me. Here is how he praises the Quarter Horse:

A Quarter Horse, in my eyes, is a performance horse; the greatest and most versatile equine the world has ever known. He can turn, slide and spin in a reining class like a ballet dancer, or he can float like a soft summer breeze in a pleasure class. He's a child's horse, a rope horse, a cutting horse who has no equal. He's got cow sense and common sense, and a proper disposition that sets him apart from other breeds. This is the Quarter Horse I know, love and respect, and I fear we are losing him.

Today there is a trend which is diluting the working Quarter Horse. It manifests itself by two extremes—stuffed horses who stand like statues and gaunt greyhounds who outrun the wind. While I have no quarrel with the halter classes or racing, I am concerned with the extremists of these divisions who are developing horses which are bred only to be led

Don Dodge rode the great mare, Poco Lena, to many a cattle-cutting championship at some of the largest shows in the Southwest.

The outstanding professional calf and steer roper, Dale Smith, started his daughter out early on the backs of his good rope horses.

and never ridden, or those whose horses are outbreeding the Thoroughbred in lack of brains and insufficient stock horse agility.

I like to think that the true beauty of a horse is found only in motion,
and that the true greatness of the Quarter Horse are those characteristics
of conformation and manners which set him apart from the Thoroughbred
and others. These admirable characteristics alone permitted him to be
registered as a distinct breed in the first place.

As I have pointed out, forerunners of the American Quarter Horse
landed in Jamestown, Virginia, with the settling colonists in 1607.
These horses and later importations were individuals of Oriental blood
that were put to work. They were not "play" horses, for racing did not
start in the colonies until later. They were workhorses; they were used
as saddle horses, pack horses, and wagon horses.

By 1656, towns had been built, trails and roads had been carved out
of the wilderness, crops had been established, and families had been
reared. There then was time for pleasure, hobbies, and play—time for
racing. And the English importations crossed with native Spanish
stock produced these straightaway speed demons.

So, I again emphasize, the early-day Quarter Horses were both using
horses and playing horses—particularly racing horses. Like the breeders of today, the colonists bred for short speed with the best stock
available. They probably did not much care what the horses looked
like, just so they were able to burn a hole in the wind. As Tom Fuller
suggests, there are still such speed-minded breeders today. But racing,
short or long, is a sport, and the fastest horses are the winners.

It is not the purpose of this book to feed the fires of controversy
by suggesting how racehorses should be bred and what they should
look like when they are mature. The fact is that the Quarter Horse
started as a racehorse and is continuing as such. And the sport of
racing—a jockey on a swift-moving equine—is one of those marvelous
sights in the world of sports.

The big game of polo, on the long field, played by high-goal athletes
atop Quarter Horses or Thoroughbreds, is also one of the all-time
great sports ever devised by man. It combines two elements prized by
man: horsemanship and a ball game. And without the rider, polo
would be nothing; there would be no game. There are other polo
games—arena polo and cowboy polo—that are fun to play on horses
of lesser quality. It is all relative, but nevertheless you still have to
have *a rider* for any of these games.

Of all the split-second contests engaged in by man and horse, I
feel that calf roping is the most rewarding to watch. In calf roping,

A pretty girl riding a beautifully conformed Quarter Horse is one of the nicest sights in the world of equine sports and exhibits. *Courtesy C. H. and Eva M. Potts.*

two athletes perform. The rope horse must be just as well coordinated and responsive as the roper. The horse must start quickly from a flat-footed stance, he must move out and follow the calf, he must rate his own speed with that of the calf. All these movements of the horse are enhanced by the man on his back.

Cattle cutting is one of those rare events that a horse truly enjoys. I do not think that he particularly likes being pulled around in a hackamore or bit, or enjoys stopping as fast as he can behind a calf and then backing up. But he does love to chase—and to block—fast-moving cattle critters.

Women on horses are very classy. They make a nice appearance in English equitation, over hunt and jump courses, and in western horsemanship and western pleasure events. Another event that is supercharged with showmanship is the barrel-racing contest against a stopwatch. To begin with it is both exciting and colorful. The ladies wear bright shirts, bell bottoms, scarves, hats, boots, knee pads, and shin guards. And they have found, because of intense competition, that they need very fast horses, either Quarter Horses or Thoroughbred-Quarter Horse crosses. Such mounts are assiduously trained to turn speedily and to cut corners as closely as possible without overturning the barrels that dot the racecourse. How some of them can make these sharp turns and still keep their four legs beneath them is a mystery. But they do it with very few falls.

Many horse shows have learned through the years that they cannot get away with just halter classes for Quarter Horses if they want to draw any kind of an attendance. They have learned that they must put men and women in the saddle. Events with riders are called *performance contests* by the AQHA, as opposed to *halter classes*, in which horses are judged solely on the basis of their conformation.

There is a place, in truth, for both events in all horse shows. But the interest and excitement will ordinarily be generated by the action—roping, reining, cow horse racing, cattle cutting, barrel running, and various other in-the-saddle contests, and all of these performances will be further explored in subsequent chapters.

3
Some Thoughts about Horse Shows

Because there are more using, riding, and pleasure horses in this country today than ever before, there are also more horse shows being conducted than ever before.

Rodeos, like the big one each summer at Salinas, California, now have performance classes in conjunction with the arena events. The gigantic livestock expositions such as Ak-Sar-Ben, in Omaha, the New Mexico State Fair, at Albuquerque, and San Francisco's Cow Palace extravaganza—all have a place for the show horse. And there are hundreds of little shows, too, privately or cooperatively produced for the benefit of certain groups or localities. Yes, sir, the horse show is here to stay. From Great Falls to Houston, from Red Bluff to Cape May!

But if you, as a Quarter Horse admirer, decide to produce or assist in producing a show, be sure you know what you are doing before the clock rolls around to the final hour . . . and there is no backing out. Do not put on a show that might evoke the following reaction from an exhibitor:

Editor, S—— News,
My letter is written concerning the Gold Coast Circuit Quarter Horse Show held in S—— on Sunday, Jan. 23.
First of all, the directions given on our printed matter were wrong. The directions led us west of the Turnpike to a Layton road which, of course, was wrong. After finally arriving at the right place, there were no accommodations for the horses, such as stalls. There was word of a breakfast given across the road at the Agricultural Center, but we did not intend to leave our horses alone at the arena site to go. The entire day's events dragged unbelievably slow. By two in the afternoon all the desserts were gone, and by five there was no Coke to drink. The only thing that kept

us going was the food concession, but no sweets or drinks (unless you like coffee). It seemed that no one was interested enough to go out and obtain more of anything to sell. I'll bet I could have sold 100 boxes of Hershey bars and many packs of cigarettes! Someone missed a golden opportunity to make money for their organization.

All through the day the announcer, whom I believe was a local veterinarian, told the western pleasure classes to "canter" their horses, which led us to believe that he was not too familiar with the difference in English riding and western riding.

Darkness came, and no lights for the arena had been provided! This was unforgivable in our opinion. The western pleasure class was quite large, and I don't see how the judge could really see how any one person handled their horse in the dark!

I should think that a small town such as S—— could benefit immensely from an event such as the horse show, but I for one and our group from Illinois will never return, and from the conversation overheard from many others we are in the majority.

Thank you very much.

B—— H——

Springfield, Ill.

The above letter, taken word for word from the S—— *News*, is reprinted here to emphasize some of the things *not* to do if you should find yourself chairman of your own local horse show committee.

And, conversely, some of the things *to* do follow: rent an adequate sound system and hire a personable announcer; if the show is apt to run into darkness, arena lights should be installed or, better still, an arena with lights already installed should be chosen; hire the services of a nationally known Quarter Horse judge or a respected local horseman who has had judging experience; from the above letter we know there are exhibitors with a sweet tooth, so arrange for a complete variety of concessions, and do not run out even if you have to make emergency trips for additional food or beverages; your show should have an arena boss and he should try at all costs to keep the show moving on schedule; if you have printed brochures or programs, they should be attractive and *correct;* have enough help on the committee so that a few people do not have to do it all before and during the show; get AQHA approval for your show; and by all means learn from past mistakes so you will not repeat your mistakes the following year. Like everything else in the Quarter Horse game, shows should be fun— for both management and labor—and they should always be organized as carefully as possible.

A word of advice: nothing suceeds like success. Think about this when you visit other Quarter Horse shows. And you should attend them. You should go to as many as you can, as an exhibitor and/or

Quarter Horse foals are tough. Here, mares and yearling colts and fillies are brought into the Buenos Aires Ranch corrals, near Sasabe, Arizona, after running on pasture for twelve months. Some of these youngsters may be blue-ribbon show horses someday.

a spectator. In this way, you can take notes on horse show merits and blunders and add them to or omit them from your own imminent horse show program.

Good luck to you from the administrative side of the business. Now let's open the barn door and saddle old Peanut Butter to ride the show circuit as a performer or exhibitor. But first let's figure out just what we are going to get out of it all. We already know it is going to cost a pretty penny to travel and haul those horses around. Are we going to benefit enough to offset this cost?

We cannot possibly make all the shows, even if we want to or can afford to. So we look at our livestock calendar (found in all horse publications) and decide on those we want to attend. This one might be fun for the kids; that one would give the wife a chance to visit her Aunt Rose; but at this other one you could see old man Ramirez about that ranch he wants to lease. You decide on "the other one." And you decide on a lot more before you put the *Quarter Horse Journal* down and go to bed. (The *Journal* is the official publication of the AQHA.)

You get to thinking about horse shows—about the nice things concerning them. You have heard the bad things before: how useless they are, the part "horse" politics plays in them, how pointless they are, the bad judging. You have heard it all. But now you think about the good things at a horse show.

Quarter Horse shows are important, you decide. Shows are the display windows of certain breeding programs and of certain areas of the country. Shows give a man an opportunity to compare and study different stallions and different bloodlines from a number of states.

At horse shows you see and talk to horsemen with the same interests as yours but perhaps with different approaches. So by keeping your eyes and ears open, you are bound to learn something from your travels. You might do a thing a certain way in your part of the country.

Many thousands of Quarter Horses, like this bunch, are taken to shows all over the country. Including stallions and mares, colts and fillies, there are more halter horses than any other kind.

Buck Adams, from up north, might do the same thing a different way, a cheaper way, a way that had never occurred to you before. You talk to him about it between classes; you talk to some other fellows about it during the classes. Suddenly you discover a way to save six hundred dollars a year. Is this show paying off for you?

If you are a relatively new breeder, raising horses to sell, it is imperative that you "hit the show circuit," so you can put your stock and your name before the horse-buying public's eye. As a general rule, most newcomers to the business of breeding horses do not sell many by just staying home. But by getting out into the horse world, they can show people what they have got. And this also is a direct means of advertising to buyers at that particular show and to persons reading the results of that show in the many livestock magazines.

Older breeders, too, in the market to sell horses, should partake of as many shows as they can conveniently squeeze into a busy life. This is the best way of showing people not only what you have in the way of breeding stock, but also exactly what that breeding stock is producing in the way of young foals. And who knows? You may sell a couple of your equine youngsters right there on the spot.

But remember, to be successful about this business you have got to be organized. Your horses have to be registered; your stock trailers or vans have to be licensed (serviced, too, before starting out); your route should be well mapped out beforehand; your entry fees and stall applications should be in on time; your equipment should be in good condition; your horses must be in good shape; and you, yourself, should feel like traveling. One other thing: if you are going into a new state, check to see what papers (hauling permit, health certificate, etc.) you will need at state border inspection stations.

When you get to the show grounds remember that the needs of your horse come first. If you are a good horseman you know this already, and you find stalls and bed your horses down with feed and water. When you have finished your horse chores, then you can go out and fetch that bottle of beer for yourself.

During the show, you "stand your horse up" on all four feet (make him look alert), so that he will attract the judge's eye. You follow the judge's instructions to the letter and you try to follow all the basic rules of good horsemanship and good showmanship.

As you leave the show, with maybe several ribbons, you think back and marvel at the wonderful organization of it, the friendliness of the show officials, the social activities, the splendid judging, and the good management. If humanly possible, you and your new-found friends will be back to that same show next year.

This is the way to have a heap of fun along with thousands of other owners and breeders who make the show circuit every year. For you surely will not keep your stallion or mare locked up in the barn. Try showing them. And by showing them, you will learn more about them, more about other horses, more about human nature and people themselves. Shows are played for everybody's benefit. Let's take advantage of them.

4
In Defense of Good Looks

In recent years it has become fashionable for some horsemen to belittle the *looks* of Quarter Horses. And some fellows, too, with a yen for scrambling words together, have written some pretty harsh lines about this superbly constructed animal.

The Quarter Horse, as many people see him—I do not say all, but many—is a gorgeous animal, a rather chubby, well-filled-out equine whose bones are covered with firm layers of flesh and muscle, on top of which is attached a sleek-haired hide. The Quarter Horse, as most people see him, is a little bit exaggerated, a little *more so* in shape and form than really need be, like a lady wrestler or a buxom Las Vegas chorus girl standing beside the average girl next door.

The Quarter Horse is usually a shiny, well-groomed creature, flawless at casual glance and almost beyond criticism in his owner's mind and eye. This attitude toward a horse is representative of horse owners and horse lovers the country over. Pride of ownership is justified as long as your pride does not hurt the other fellow or get you into trouble. Pride of ownership is firmly rooted in the Quarter Horse industry and, I believe, helps the business.

I get angry when I hear somebody put down conformation breeders and the results of their efforts. Conformation breeders would not be striving for *horse appearance* unless they were proud of what they were doing and felt justified in doing it.

If you hark back to the early days of the AQHA, you will recall that the men who founded the organization were men who favored appearance in a horse. Above all else—action and bloodlines included—they were interested in perpetuating a certain type. They may not have

A Quarter Horse stallion exercising in a paddock is a beautiful sight as he runs free of any restraint.

been one hundred percent right; neither were they one hundred percent wrong. They knew what they were after and they strove and fought to preserve those traits which they thought belonged to a true Quarter Horse. In so doing they may have overemphasized certain characteristics of conformation, but they were sincere in their beliefs.

Today it is popular among certain groups of modern breeders to lambaste the founding fathers of the AQHA and to hint broadly that they raised nothing but a bunch of overfed, worthless horses. This is not right. Especially in a breed that is so young. For there is the distinct possibility that in years to come, another group of breeders will be lambasting the current efforts of our contemporary horsemen. Everyone is, of course, entitled to his own opinion. But thoughtless criticism, just for its own sake, is harmful to the other fellow, to the breed itself, and, indirectly, to the critics.

Quarter Horses have always evoked controversy, and always will. Good, clean, healthy controversy is fine, but when men are cruel to each other and each other's horseflesh, their differences of opinion have gone too far. I think they have gone too far today when some horsemen undermine the faith and love other horsemen have for a certain kind or type of horse—a certain kind of good looks. Admittedly, the emphasis today is toward action and performance. I personally like performance and think all horses should be bred with some type of action in mind. But why consistently fault the man who breeds with appearance only in mind? Instead, let's respect his aims, even though we do not agree with them.

Quarter Horse men are, in general, pretty stubborn hombres. No matter what sort of horse they like, no matter what kind of activity they prefer, no matter what bloodlines they specialize in, once they get a notion fixed in their head, that notion is there to stay for a while. Several horsemen can get together to argue all night long, but with the coming of dawn each of them will invariably depart with the same ideas, the same convictions, the same personal opinions that he carried into the fray.

The man who breeds for looks in a horse is usually referred to as a *halter* man or a *conformation* man. And let's not forget that the first formal competition, after the AQHA was organized, was this type of show with a designated judge to pick the winners. A conformation man may not give a hoot about how fast a Quarter Horse can run a quarter of a mile; he may not care how quickly a Quarter Horse can catch a calf; he neither raves about the clod-scattering stops and turns of a cutting horse, nor dissolves into a puddle of emotion when he hears about the faithfulness of Old Sabado out on the range. He might say, "See here now, neighbor, this horse of yours is no darn good. All he can do is run the quarter in twenty-two flat. What good does that do anybody? And look at your old pony—a bag of bones . . . a coat rack of nervous indigestion . . . a skeleton of jumps and starts . . . fits and flaps. There sure must be something better to do with a horse." But he probably says nothing, so, in all fairness, action breeders should refrain from disparaging horses that are bred entirely for good looks.

The conformation breeder is also a specialist, just as much as the racehorse breeder, the cutting horse breeder, or the ranch horse breeder. He specializes in bone and muscle and shape; he specializes in certain types of heads, in wide rumps, in a strong "V" between the forelegs, in sturdy, sloping shoulders, and in muscular forearms and gaskins. He specializes in producing a show horse. And he feeds and grooms this horse until it is in show shape (fatter than most working horses, it is true), and then he exhibits his horse on a halter shank before a judge.

This is his way in the game of Quarter Horses. This is his *thing*. It is a way that other horsemen should not harshly criticize. For within the Quarter Horse business there is great diversity. There exists the possibility of doing just about anything and everything a person can do with or on a horse.

Jack Kurtz, Oklahoma rancher, holds the well-muscled Quarter Horse stud, Major Thunder, in a pose that would please the most persnickety of judges.

5
Know Your Quarter Horse Markings

Do you ever get befuddled on the exact nomenclature for the markings on a horse's face or leg (below the knee or hock)? "Heck, no!" you will probably answer. "That's pretty elementary stuff." But occasionally you will hear somebody—maybe a person tall in the saddle—get all mixed up describing a horse's color or its markings.

So for the edification of readers who may want to recheck the various markings of face and foot, take a look at the accompanying illustrations by John Mariani, whose task it was some years ago to draw these examples for the AQHA. They were—and are—to be used as a guide by breeders when making applications for Quarter Horse registry.

And with the drawings, here are the following brief descriptions of these markings:

BALD: A very broad blaze. It can extend out and around the eyes and down to the upper lip and around the nostrils.

BLAZE: A broader, more open stripe.

CORONET: Any narrow marking around the coronet above the hoof.

HALF PASTERN: A marking that includes only half the pastern above the coronet.

PASTERN: A marking that includes the entire pastern.

SNIP: Any marking, usually vertical, between the two nostrils.

SOCK: A marking that extends around the leg from the coronet halfway up the cannon bone, or halfway to the knee on the foreleg or halfway to the hock on the back leg.

STAR: Any marking on the forehead.

STAR AND STRIPE: A marking on the forehead with a stripe to the nasal peak. The stripe does not have to be an extension of the star.

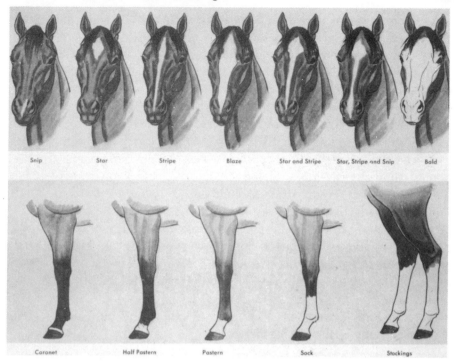

Snip   Star   Stripe   Blaze   Star and Stripe   Star, Stripe and Snip   Bald

Coronet   Half Pastern   Pastern   Sock   Stockings

Quarter Horse markings. Courtesy John Mariani and AQHA.

STAR, STRIPE, AND SNIP: A marking on the forehead with a narrow extension to the nasal peak and opening up again between the nostrils.

STOCKING: A full marking almost to the knee on the foreleg and almost to the hock on the hind leg. It is an extended sock.

STRIPE: A long vertical marking running down the entire length of the face from forehead to nasal peak.

You may also want to refresh your memory concerning some Quarter Horse color schemes. Here they are as designated by the AQHA.

BAY: Body color ranging from tan, through red, to reddish brown; mane and tail black; usually black on lower legs.

BLACK: Body color true black without light areas; mane and tail black.

BLUE ROAN: Body color more or less a uniform mixture of white and black hairs, usually with a few red hairs.

BROWN: Body color brown or black with light areas at muzzle, eyes, flank, and inside upper legs; mane and tail black; usually black on lower legs.

BUCKSKIN: A form of dun with body color yellowish or gold; mane and tail black, usually black on lower legs.

CHESTNUT: Body color dark red or reddish-brown; mane and tail usually same color as body, but may be flaxen.

DUN: Body color yellowish or gold; mane and tail may be black, brown, red, yellow, white or mixed; often has dorsal stripe, zebra stripes on legs, and transverse stripe over withers.

GRAY: Body color a mixture of black and white hairs; usually born solid colored or almost solid colored and gets lighter with age.

GRULLO: Body color smoky or mouse colored (not a mixture of black and white hairs, but with each hair mouse colored); mane and tail black; usually black on lower legs.

PALOMINO: Body color a golden yellow; mane and tail white.

RED DUN: A form of dun with body color yellowish or flesh colored, mane and tail red, dorsal stripe.

RED ROAN: Body color more or less a uniform mixture of white and red hairs.

SORREL: Body color reddish or copper-red; mane and tail usually same color as body, but may be flaxen.

6
Indoor, Outdoor, and Cowboy Polo

Six mallet-swinging riders raced down the field, reining their horses to proper positions behind and around the hard-hit polo ball. They did not have far to go. The shot caromed off the side boards and the ball skittered in front of the goal. Attacking players stormed in, trying to make the point. Defensive players also converged on the ball, trying to block the point.

All six ponies were pulled up against or near the boards. In the hot scramble that followed, the heavy blow of breathless horses and the sharp cracking of mallet blocking mallet sounded like a forest fire. Then an alert backhand shot slammed the ball home. The referee blew his whistle, indicating a tally had been scored, and the two teams lined up again in the center of the field to resume play.

"This is polo?" an excited spectator asked as he watched his first "indoor" or "arena" competition. "It looks more like basketball on horseback." And these words might well be the most accurate yet to describe the quick-action teamwork and speedy maneuvering in the miniature matches that are currently being played in the western states.

Indoor polo, actually played in buildings like the Essex Troop Hall in West Orange, New Jersey, and the Squadron "A" Armory in New York City, has been popular for years in the East with both amateur and professional malletmen. So-called indoor polo in the West is fairly new and is held, despite its deceiving name, outdoors.

But the most astonishing thing about this kind of polo is that the preferred horse is the Quarter Horse and not the Thoroughbred, which has been the number one choice of polo players for years. The main reason for the popularity of the Quarter Horse in the small game

Indoor, or arena, polo is played throughout the Southwest in enclosed arenas like this one. Most of the horses are Quarter Horses.

is the size of the arena or boarded-in area. A typical one will measure only 100 yards long by 50 yards wide. Now compare this to the regulation outdoor polo field, which is 300 yards long—three times the distance of a football field—by 150 yards wide.

Quarter Horses, having been bred for quick starts, early speed, and lateral maneuverability, find the small field to their liking. They can make these moves better than the Thoroughbred, which has been for centuries bred and trained to run long distances. But it should be added here, to placate the big-game polo player, that the Thoroughbred is still the best horse for the long game, although Thoroughbreds of the Quarter Horse type are found in many top polo strings all over the world.

Arena-type fields are either dirt or grass. Some are open-ended, some are closed, boarded five feet high all the way around. Some are further enclosed by an additional six feet of meshed wire fencing held upright by spaced poles. The vertically striped, boarded goal of closed-

Jack Bowman, riding a Quarter Horse, is about to clobber the ball in a polo arena near Tucson, Arizona. Joe Lane, on the gray Thoroughbred, tries to ride him off the ball. *Courtesy Wong.*

Jack Moore sits astride a very good example of the polo pony type of Quarter Horse. The horse is fast and alert and can turn and spin on a dime.

end fields is ten feet square, compared to the twenty-four-foot goal mouth of outdoor polo.

Within this rectangular boundary, curved at the corners, a bouncy, leather-covered ball, with an inflated rubber lining, is constantly in motion. In fierce pursuit are the six horsemen who play in the indoor game, instead of the eight men in outdoor polo. Successful defensive strategy depends on how efficiently opponents are "ridden off," shots are blocked, and positions are retained. Quick-thinking cooperation on the offensive, with lots of short passes, is mandatory.

For onlookers who have difficulty in following the larger game, the indoor version is concentrated into close focus. Even some top-ranking outdoor players, who admit that the "tiny game" takes more skill and fancier stick work, have been converted to arena polo.

The arena game is not one of long, smashing hits and straightaway dashes down the length of the field, as is the regular polo game. The ball, about the size of a grapefruit, is put into play in the center of the arena, tossed by the referee into the center of the opposing teams' lineups. The No. 1 players will try to tip the ball in the throw-in, sending it down field toward their opponent's goal. If this happens, a quick burst of speed is desired from the horse ridden by the No. 1 who has hit the ball. His business is to overtake the rolling ball and hit it again. His opponent's business is to get there first, ride the offensive No. 1 off the ball, and attempt a backshot toward the other goal or to one of his teammates.

In the West (Arizona, California, Texas, and Wyoming), where most small-game arenas are found, Quarter Horses are meeting the test with much success and a lot of get-up-and-go. One Quarter Horse riding mallet man put it this way: "When I show my horse a hole the size of a needle head, I want him to go through it—and I want him to go through it right now, not next week."

Still another polo game in which Quarter Horses are used is called cowboy polo. It is played for the most part in Texas, New Mexico, Arizona, Colorado, and Florida, where a similar version is known as palmetto polo. Western saddles are used along with western bits and bridles. Riders' uniforms are plain old cowboy clothes, so the game is very informal.

Because it is played on a field split into five zones, cowboy polo is hard on neither man nor horse. And that is why it is popular as a riding club or sheriff's posse recreation. It is a game of action, even though riders cannot leave their zones, since every zone gets some flurry of activity as the basketball-sized ball bounds up and down the field.

Each zone contains two players, one from each team. The players battle, combining skillful stick work and horsemanship, for control of the ball. The one that gets control tries to whop the ball into another zone, but always headed for the opponents' goal. If the ball successfully passes through the zones and is lobbed into a goal, a score is chalked up.

7
Quarter Horses Will Be Your Friends

I have heard people say that they do not trust horses, that they do not feel at ease around them. Ninety-nine times out of one hundred this distrust is unfounded. For if a horse is broken and trained correctly, he will be very trustworthy. He will do his best to work as you want him to. In short, he will be your friend. Quarter Horses, because of their gentle dispositions and intelligence, are very good horses to have as friends.

Perhaps this was not so twenty-five or fifty years ago, when horses were broken and trained quickly and sometimes thoughtlessly. Some horses in those days were one-man mounts and had to be strong-armed every time they were ridden.

I once asked an old-time Oklahoma cowboy and rodeo roper how he would suggest putting a stop on a young Quarter Horse I had started to train for the arena. "There's just one way to do it," he said. "Get you a big, stout, fast-running cow. Then you take after this cow on your colt, having in mind to rope her. When you reach her, throw your rope and whop it on her. Then get off quick like. The first thing that'll hit the ground will be the saddle horn. Gather everything up and do it again, and I'll guarantee you the third time you rope that cow, your colt's going to be ready. He'll be watching. He'll prop his legs; he'll stop good—and he sure won't be jerked down any more."

There are words of wisdom here, but I wonder how many current trainers are tempted to train a prospective rope horse in this rough-and-tumble manner. A good colt might be permanently crippled or badly rope burned. A trainer might also break his own neck.

There are easier ways to train your horse to stop behind a cow brute

The young lady, typical of many who visit the dude ranches of the West each year, has made a friend of her Quarter-type horse from the dude riders' string. *Courtesy Chuck Abbott.*

(these will be discussed in a later chapter), and, I think, a horse will appreciate a milder lesson. He will be more of a friend if you teach him to stop easily and slowly on light calves instead of starting him out and jerking him down on seven-hundred- to nine-hundred-pound cows.

Most western horsemen do not make pets of their horseflesh. Neither do they abuse them in breaking, training, showing, or specialty riding. If you have "light hands" on the reins and if you sit erect and balanced in the saddle, sooner or later, somehow, your horse is going to let you know that he is aware of your good horsemanship.

When a colt is first started out he is naturally scared. If he has been running loose with his mother away from people and man-made contrivances, he will be terrified when you first start to fool with him. So no matter what you try doing with him first—whip breaking, halter breaking, or general handling—you have got to gain his confidence. You have got to make him understand that you are not going to hurt him.

Colts that have been around people, in pastures or stalls or paddocks, are usually pretty gentle and, after weaning, are easy to halter break. They may or may not be easy to saddle, depending on the individual.

John Hazelwood, long-time racehorse trainer, let his race prospects break themselves. He once said: "I saddle a colt with an exercise saddle and just let him walk around in a stall for three or four days. Then I have a jockey get on him and walk and turn and back the colt for another day. The next day I have the jockey ride the horse out of the stall. We very seldom see a horse that'll buck after this treatment."

Hazelwood, who used to train for the Finley Ranches of Arizona, told me that this was the way the two fine mares, Bardella and Little Egypt, were started.

It really does not make much difference what you are breaking and training a horse to be. If you are mild and calm, he will be a better horse. Hazelwood went easy with his charges. So should you.

The first thing a horse breaker usually does, after gaining his colt's confidence (which generally means that he is halter broken and no longer frightened of it or you), is to take an old sack or saddle blanket and flop it all over the colt for several days, or until the colt stands perfectly still no matter where the blanket is put.

Then you can either pull up a hind leg or hobble the forelegs with strong, soft (sometimes braided) cotton rope, thereby making sure that your colt will stay put when you ease the saddle on him. After the saddle is on, cinched down fairly tightly, you can slowly swing up into it if the colt is gentle enough.

The late King Merritt of Wyoming has pulled the bit and bridle off Powderhorn, and the Quarter Horse gelding seems to be enjoying the prospect of preventing the boy from passing him on either side. *Courtesy Orren Mixer.*

If you think the colt will fight or struggle and perhaps fall down, you will do better by freeing his legs and mounting while another rider snubs your colt to his saddle.

But if you have taken a long time with your colt, he should be docile enough to climb aboard with his forelegs hobbled. Get on and off many times—from both near and off sides. Rub the colt down with your hands and slap him all over. Get him used to your sitting up there on top of him.

Remember in this operation—as in all others before and after—you are still trying to gain more and more of your horse's confidence. At this stage of breaking, you are striving to make him understand that these strange antics will not hurt him.

When you start riding the horse, it is best to have somebody pony you for a day or two—until he gets used to seeing the world with you on his back. If you have a good solid breaking pen, you can start riding him here. Once he is gentle under saddle, you can start training him in any way you like.

It is not the purpose of this chapter to set forth any hard and fast rules about breaking and training. I have mentioned some rather elementary ideas for exemplary purposes only. Everybody has his own ideas about breaking and training.

The one important thought, however, that everybody should keep in mind and should follow is this: your horse is going to appreciate you more and be a better horse for you if you treat him kindly and with the utmost patience when he is a colt. If you will be his friend, he will be yours.

8
How to Rope and Tie a Calf

A lot of people rope and tie calves. Calf roping can be sport, recreation, profession, pastime, or vocation, and on top of all this it is also a means of enjoying good Quarter Horses and projecting one's own horsemanship and training talents toward a very rewarding end.

I knew a fellow once who never won a dime at a first-rate rodeo, yet he was an avid roping enthusiast. His pleasure came not in competition and winning big purses, but in training horses. He put everything he knew into schooling his ponies, and when he had one perfectly "made," he would immediately lose all interest in that horse. He would then sell it to make room for another "green" horse, which he would start to train. And this went on all year around.

So roping means different things to different people. The pleasure from its end results can vary greatly with the individual person. The professional roper is seriously after the cold cash. Nothing gives him a greater thrill than bringing home a bundle of greenbacks. The semi-pro roper likes to win, too, but to him roping may be more of a game. The amateur ropes strictly for enjoyment and recreation. And then, like our friend, there are those who find the most challenging and rewarding aspect of roping in the schooling of the horse.

Roping is fun. In addition to the large following of ropers in the ranks of the Rodeo Cowboys Association (the professional cowboys' union), there are also college and high school rodeo teams, with calf roping as the main event. There are hundreds of roping clubs spread out across the country. Sheriffs' posses and riding groups can also usually boast of some top ropers. Small amateur rodeos at dude ranches and similar resorts program roping as one of the most popular events at ranch rodeos. Special contests and matched ropings appeal to the

Frank Owenby pops his loop on a running calf and prepares to wave the slack rope away in front, as the buckskin Quarter Horse starts to apply the brakes.

tophand pros throughout the West. And now in recent years, such pros as Toots Mansfield, Don McLaughlin, Jim Bob Altizer, Glen Franklin, and Dean Oliver conduct schools of roping instruction.

Anyone with the slightest degree of coordination can learn to rope. The popular appeal lies in the fact that you do not have to be a cowboy to be a good roper. Many city-reared fellows snare plenty of roping money on the rodeo circuits each year.

The late, great bronc rider, Jerry Ambler, once told me that he thought top bronc riders had to be born that way, like musicians or singers, but that folks who have a yen to rope could develop themselves by application and practice, by a thorough knowledge of how to ride and train a rope horse, and by having good horses to rope on.

The best roping horse in the world, however, is not going to run out and do the job for you. This you have got to do yourself. So let's find out how you are going to go about snagging that junior Brahman.

To begin with get those kinks out of your rope, which should be about twenty-four to twenty-five feet long, and adjust it to the saddle, remembering to run it through the neck rope. You should always work with a neck rope, especially if you are training a green horse or your mount is inclined to be a little spooky. It is embarrassing to be asked over for an evening of roping by a friend and end up choking his baby steers simply because you have not got any restraining string around Old Pal's neck.

Now shake out a loop and into the chute you go. Before giving the nod to the barrier man, make dead certain everything is in working order. That all-important loop should be free from twists, and there should be ample room between the coils in your left hand and the loop in your right hand so that your swing is not forced or crowded. The

Calf roping and tying is so much fun that they really start 'em young in the West!

balance (from where you hold the loop to where the rope runs through the honda) should equal about one-half the size of the loop when it is held at arm's length. At all times your rope should feel right to you. You should be able to swing it with an easy, natural motion without its becoming fouled or kinked in any way. When it gets all wound up in everything but the calf's head, you are not adjusting it to the saddle properly. Nobody ever caught anything with a rope that did not move out fast or a loop that did not open.

Now you are all set and the barrier is released. Provided that horse of yours is no beginner, you will be within throwing distance of your quarry in five to eight seconds.

When you send that loop out toward its mark, remember that there is the equivalent of a stiff wind blowing at you head on. If you do not throw with speed and strength, the loop will wad up in the air before it ever reaches the calf's ears. So throw a fast, snappy loop. Beginners should try to place a flat loop in front of the calf in such a position that the animal, if it runs straight, will stick its head right into the circle. After some experience, you can begin spot-looping your calves and bailing out of the saddle as you toss the slack.

But whoa! I'm getting a little bit ahead of myself. What about throwing that loop? You may not realize it but throwing a catch-loop at a calf's head is much the same as pitching a baseball across the plate. Both throws get accuracy and force behind them with a simple snap-wrist motion and follow through. Try throwing your rope as if it were a baseball some time when you are practicing on the ground. Then take a ball and throw it at a target on the ground with the same motion you would use tossing a rope. You will see the similarity and it is bound to help the roper whose loop is forever landing on the backs of fast-running calves.

After you catch your calf—the right way is clean around the neck—there are a number of ways and styles of pitching the slack rope. The purpose of this procedure is to prevent your horse from running over the rope with his forelegs. Each roper has his own particular way of getting rid of the slack before or as he steps off. The most common and easiest method is to throw it away in front of you.

As you do so, try getting off like this: the moment you pitch the slack, grasp the saddle horn with your right hand and reach far up on your horse's neck with your left hand. Now just swing off as your horse stops and you will note that you are very well balanced, braced three ways—by your two arms and your left foot in the stirrup.

This method is also a signal to the horse to stop when he feels the extra weight on his neck. It is also an excellent way to train a young

Old Sea Biscuit, a New Mexico rope horse, was made the way the cowboys like to see 'em. This good roan gelding could run and stop and
turn—all desirable traits of a top rope horse.

horse without pulling his mouth out of shape. If you need to yank the
horse up once in a while, you can as you get off by pulling on the rein
instead of pushing on his neck. A horse that is trained to stop on a
loose rein will work far better, in the long run, than one that will not
put on the brakes until he feels the bit tighten up.

After you have caught the calf, flipped away the slack in the rope,
and stepped off, the most important part of making fast time lies
ahead. True, you have to catch the calf before you can tie it, but if
you catch it and cannot tie it you are in a bad spot, too!

As you start down the rope after your calf, grab the rope and let
it slide between your arm and side—like a guideline. Wherever the
calf goes you will be heading in the right direction. When you reach
the animal you will have your right hand on the honda to steady the
calf until you snatch up its right foreleg. As soon as you have control

grab that front leg with both hands and pull upward. At the same time throw your left hip or knee into its flank. If it is a jumping calf, it will usually flip itself to the ground when you apply the pressure.

Now, still keeping a hold on the right leg so the calf cannot get up, jump quickly over the animal's body, so that you are standing at its back, and pop your pigging string on that same right front leg. Pull it tight and throw the end off to the side out of the way. Then gather up the two hind legs, crossing them over the same foreleg, and start to wrap, remembering that you will not go to the pay window if the calf shakes the wraps loose. On a tough, kicking calf, make sure that your first wrap is tight and secure. Then go for speed on your next wrap and your tuck or half hitch.

No hard and fast rules apply to tying. Each roper, by trial and error, will eventually work out a tie that is right for him. But remember this: the professional ropers—the best in the world—are beating one another on the ground and not on horseback. They all rope about the same and they are all superbly mounted. On the ground, getting "the jump 'n' the tie" on the big calves, is where the money is won.

As in any other athletic event where a certain skill is required, roping calves well takes lots of practice. Good rodeo ropers work at it all they can, roping all day long at home when they are not on the circuit. The late Jake McClure, one of the greatest of calf ropers, was always handling a rope. No one ever saw Jake any place in the arena, mounted or on foot, without his rope, swinging it or dabbing it on this or that. Such devotion to rope work and practice not only paid off for Jake McClure, but is paying off for many of the fastest boys in the business today. Take your rope down off your saddle and keep it active. Practice can pay off for you, too!

9
Speed, Speed, and More Speed

"Off with the horse collar . . . and on with the jockey," somebody suggested at the 1950 AQHA national convention. And much to the outrage of breeders who were raising slow but pretty horses, and who then thought these were the only kind to raise, the speed boom was born.

Two years later, in the November issue of the *Quarter Horse Journal,* I wrote an editorial that said:

> Quarter Horse racing is still on the up-jump and, we believe, it can be expected to keep on mounting in popularity—a popularity Quarter racing enjoys not only with the owners and trainers, but with the wagering public as well.
>
> It has been said that the average race goer prefers the Thoroughbred or distance race, wherein he gets "more of a run for his money." This cannot be argued with, but we will say that where the betting public has been thoroughly educated to Quarter racing at some of the fairly large tracks in California, Arizona and New Mexico—then these same bettors take to the short sprints as readily as they do the longer races.

Quarter Horse racing has grown up fast. Two decades ago we used to see a few horse trailers or vans heading for the racetracks. Today hundreds of trailers and vans are constantly on the road, carrying sprint hopefuls to scores and scores of tracks—large and small—all over the country. Some very special equine speedsters are even flown from ranch to track.

The challenge and thrill of trying to produce the very fastest horses in the world (for a short distance) has given the Quarter Horse breeding fraternity something substantial to shoot at. The continuing boom

Well-bred Quarter Horses like this one can sizzle over a quarter-mile course in under twenty-two seconds.

has also created a demand for additional track personnel, jockeys, trainers, stable hands, veterinarians, farriers, and so on. The sport is big business today with big money involved.

Writing in *Quarter Racing World,* one of several publications devoted to the running Quarter Horse, publisher Walt Wiggins says:

> From 25 AQHA-recognized races in 1945, it [Quarter Horse racing] has grown to over 8,500 in 1971. The pari-mutuel handle of Quarter Horse races has soared from $6.5 million in 1951 to almost $16 million in 1971. Purse distribution to horsemen in 1951 was $363,285. In 1971 the horsemen received some $11 million more. Every graph or chart relative to the sport and industry of the running Quarter Horse has virtually shot off the board over the past 20 years.

Quarter Racing World is published in Roswell, New Mexico. Another magazine, published in Fort Worth, Texas, is called the *Quarter Racing Record.* The *Quarter Horse Journal,* based with its parent association, the AQHA, in Amarillo, Texas, publishes an annual "Racing Issue." The AQHA also puts out a monthly *Quarter Running Horse Chart Book*—a continuing official record of facts and figures from the world of short-distance running horses.

In recent years, too, in answer to the demand for material on straightaway racing, several annuals or yearbooks have appeared, jam-packed with information. They are *Quarter Racing Stakes Horses,* compiled by Renee Smelker (915 N. Barbara Worth, Tucson, Ariz. 85710); *Quarter Horse Reference* (P. O. Box 487, Grapevine, Texas 76051); the *Quarter Horse Yearbook* (503 First City National Bank Bldg., Houston, Texas 77002); and *Quarter Race Breeding Analysis* (P. O. Box 81, Monterey, Calif. 93940).

Other promotions for the good of short-horse racing are Quarter Horse Tours, organized by Roy Davis of Amarillo, former editor of the *Quarter Horse Journal,* and the National Museum of Quarter Racing at Roswell, sponsored by the Quarter Racing Owners of America.

The QROA also sponsors what it calls a "Quarter Racing Hotline." It is simply a twenty-four-hour-a-day telephone service, providing stakes race results and other news items of the industry. Two numbers are available. One number (505 623–2030) is for use by anyone having news to give to the Hotline office. The other number (505 623–1330) is for use by anyone—a newspaper reporter, for instance—wanting race results or current short-horse industry news.

The Hotline was devised, actually taken from a page in the book of harness racing, to combat the dearth of publicity that plagued the short-horse people for many years. Now in a few minutes, timely race

A tightly packed group of Quarter Horse mudders head for the wire at Tucson, Arizona's Rillito Park in a four-hundred-yard straightaway dash.

results can be received or distributed by the easy dialing of a number.

A great number of other horse and livestock magazines, both western and eastern, carry news or present features on Quarter Horse sprinters, including the *Daily Racing Form*.

Two tracks, more than any others, deserve the most credit for helping this sport grow. They are Ruidoso Downs, high in the Mescalero Mountains of southern New Mexico, and Los Alamitos, southern California's famous all-Quarter Horse racing plant. (Recently harness horses started running at Los Alamitos in a separate event.)

Ruidoso caters to both summer Thoroughbred and Quarter Horse runners. It also dishes up a very special kind of dessert, closing the season each year on Labor Day weekend with the running of the richest horse race in the entire world—the All-American Futurity for Quarter Horses. The gross purse has now reached the fantastic sum of one million dollars. The money is distributed to the owners of forty colts and fillies, two-year-olds that run in four 440-yard dashes. (The forty juveniles are selected from a series of electronically timed All-American Futurity trials.)

Ruidoso Downs is also the home of several other very rich races,

A midweek training session on how to jump from a starting gate may produce results in the three-hundred-yard race over the weekend.

including the All-American Derby at 440 yards, the Kansas Futurity at 350 yards, and the Rainbow Futurity at 400 yards. (In the event you find yourself with an exceptional foal, one that you think will burn a hole in the wind, contact Ruidoso Downs' Liz Devine, Nominations Secretary, P. O. Box 449, Ruidoso Downs, N. M. 88346.)

Los Alamitos Race Course is the dream-come-true of the late Frank Vessels, Sr. One day in 1947, he presented six races (with no betting) to a crowd of about fifteen hundred spectators in what was more or less the backyard of his ranch.

After more than three years of informal racing, the California State Racing Commission in 1951 approved an eleven-day all-Quarter Horse race meet with pari-mutuel wagering. Los Alamitos, today the biggest track in the land for these sprinters, was on its way.

The track is now ably run by the senior Vessels' son, Frank, Jr., and four-footed contenders in futurities, derbies, and maturities run for estimated purses of $150,000 instead of the $2,500 to $7,500 purses of the early days.

With Los Alamitos' thirteen- and nine-week meets, in the spring and fall, California can boast of three big Quarter Horse racing sessions—the third one is at Bay Meadows in San Mateo—and several smaller state fair meetings.

Quarter Horse meets are also now run in Kentucky, Florida, Louisiana, Oklahoma, Illinois, Utah, Ohio, New York, Michigan, Colorado, Montana, Wyoming, Arizona, Missouri, Kansas, Arkansas, South Dakota, Nevada, Indiana, and Texas. Even though Texas law prohibits pari-mutuel betting, the total purse on the Texas Quarter Horse racing circuit is estimated at close to $950,000. The circuit includes race meets at Columbus, Hilltop, Uvalde, Laredo, Goliad, Del Rio, Sonora, and Brady. Canada also has Quarter Horse racing.

Time, money, and experimentation have contributed to the extraordinary growth of Quarter Horse racing. In an effort to produce faster horses, breeders have raised some controversial issues, chief among them being the ruckus over the use of Thoroughbred blood in Quarter Horse breeding.

In this controversy I do not want to take sides. I feel, however, that the dispute has served to stimulate breeder and spectator interest in the sport, because from the experimental breeding of differing bloodlines and horse types has come many of the current racing stars that run to filled stands and fat mutuel handles.

Some breeders are still getting foals from traditionally accepted Quarter Horse bloodlines. Many of these colts and fillies make names for themselves and when they compete against "half" or "mostly" Thoroughbreds, there is bound to be a flurry of interest.

So, as we can see, the future of this straightaway sport is assured, if past performance and the continual shattering of all sorts of records mean anything at all. The business is big and it is growing bigger. Where it will stop, if it does, is anybody's guess.

10
The Finer Points of
Quarter Horse Judging

Even though I have never judged an AQHA Quarter Horse show, I have watched with interest while others officiated. Some of the famous judges I have seen at work are Roy Savage, Ray Lewis, Punk Snyder, Hugh Bennett, Tom Finley, Casey Darnell, and others. And once at Tucson's Southern Arizona International Livestock Show, I judged one class.

The late Volney Hildreth, who ranched at Aledo, Texas, was judging and I was acting as arena assistant. Along the way, Volney suddenly discovered that he was placing horses in a class that included one that he had bred.

"Porter," he said, "I never judge a class with one of my horses in it— take over!"

I guess my placings were all right. At least there was not a mob after me later on that day.

Another time at Amarillo, Texas, when I was working for the *Quarter Horse Journal*, the AQHA held a seminar for its various judges around the country. Six or seven were attending and, since I was on hand to cover the proceedings for the magazine, I was also given a judge's card and told to go to work.

The judges were practicing on a small group of geldings owned by Glen Casey, who was then famous as the owner of two top show individuals—the stallion, Bill Cody, and the mare, Jole Blon. The geldings were not in show shape. Their hair was coarse and long and they had been out to pasture.

Although the late Driftwood was a great sire of roping, bulldogging, and reining horses, he did not have "ideal" Quarter Horse conformation.

When the judging cards were compared, none of them were the same, and Ray Lewis, who was acting as moderator, chose mine as the closest best example of conformation judging. Editing a magazine was my job, not horse judging, so I mention this only to emphasize this point: *all horse conformation judging is personal opinion.*

Conformation, says the AQHA, "is the form or outline of an animal— the symmetrical arrangement of its parts." But a qualified Quarter Horse judge should have a thorough knowledge of both the skeletal and muscular structure of the animal and also know "how and why movement or restricted movement affects the usefulness of the horse in motion," again according to the AQHA.

If you should start to raise Quarter Horses, no matter in what section of the United States, and make a name for yourself as a breeder, then you will be sought after as a judge. You may not be asked to judge the really huge shows, such as Denver, Fort Worth, San Francisco, or Phoenix, but you will certainly be called on to judge some of the smaller regional shows. And if you turn out to be a popular judge at

This bulldogging horse, owned by Slim Whaley of Duncan, Oklahoma, is a very well-made sort of performance horse.

the regionals, you will probably go on—and you should go on for your own edification—to the nationals.

But before you ever get into the arena with perhaps twenty or thirty horses in one class, let's look over the following descriptive Quarter Horse judging material, reprinted here through the courtesy of the AQHA:

This is the AQHA's model horse, showing the muscle and the well-balanced conformation, and also indicating the important areas of a horse. *Courtesy AQHA.*

HEAD: The head is relatively short and wide, with a small muzzle and a shallow, firm mouth. The upper and lower teeth meet when biting. The nostrils are full and sensitive. The medium length, alert ears are set wide apart. The large eyes are also set wide; they reflect intelligence and a placid disposition. Well-developed jaws imply great strength.

NECK: The head of the Quarter Horse joins the neck at a near 45-degree angle. The throatlatch—the area between the jawbone and neck muscles—is trim, without too much thickness or depth, and there is width between the lower edges of the jaw bone to enable him to work with his head down and not restrict his breathing. The neck of sufficient length blends into sloping shoulders. The horse uses his neck as a balance, and the maneuverability of a horse depends to a large degree on the flexibility of the neck. A high-arched neck or heavy crest is undesirable.

SHOULDERS: The shoulder is long, set at an angle of about 45 degrees to give the horse a long stride; it is smooth but relatively heavy muscled. The slope of the shoulder blends into the withers. The unusually good saddle back of the Quarter Horse is created by his medium-high and well defined withers, extending back beyond the top of his shoulder so the saddle is held in proper position for balanced action. The withers and croup are approximately the same height.

CHEST AND FORELEGS: The Quarter Horse is deep and broad chested, as indicated by his great heart girth and wide-set forelegs which blend into his shoulders. The muscling on the inside of the forearm gives the appearance of a well-defined inverted V.

BACK: The short saddle-back of the Quarter Horse is close coupled and especially full and powerful across the loin. The barrel or girth is deep with well-sprung ribs. The underline, or belly, is longer than the back and does not cut high into the flank.

REAR QUARTERS: The rear quarters are broad, deep and heavy when viewed from either side or rear, and are muscled so they are full through the thigh, stifle, gaskin and down to the hock. The croup should be long and slope gently from the hip to the tail set. The loin blends into the croup. The hip muscling is long, extending down into the stifle; the stifle ties in well to the gaskin; and the gaskin muscle extends down into the hock joint, both inside and outside.

STIFLE: The stifle is deep, and when viewed from the rear, extends out below the hip and above the gaskin. When viewed from the rear the stifle is the widest part of the animal.

GASKIN: The gaskin is wide and shows a related thickness both inside and out when viewed from the rear.

HOCK: The hock is broad, flat, clean, strong, low set, and free of excess tissue. The muscling ties well into the hock joint. There is no play or give in the hock joint except directly forward.

CANNON: The cannon bones are short, with the hock and knee joints low to the ground. The cannon bones, both front and rear, show a perpendicular position and appear quite broad when viewed from the side; the tendons, back and below the knees and hocks, appear sharply separated from the bone and from each other.

ANKLE-PASTERN-HOOF: The ankle is well-formed and strong to withstand shock and strain. The medium length pasterns denote strength; they have a slightly forward slope, about 45 degrees. Viewed from either the front or rear, the legs, cannons and pasterns are straight. The hoof is oblong; its size balances with the over-all size of the individual animal; it is tough textured with a deep wide open heel and has the same slope as the pastern. The pastern must not be perpendicular. A pastern that is too straight is a conformation fault, for it generally results in irreparable damage to the movement of a horse.

SOME COMMON DEFECTS: While they are not always considered hereditary faults there are certain unsoundnesses with which a judge should be familiar; among these are bone spavin, curbs, thoroughpin, splints, wind galls, and ring bone. Although these may not be conformation faults, their presence may lead a judge to suspect an undesirable weakness. A judge, however, is not bound to fault a horse because of one or more minor defects if the animal is otherwise superior.

BALANCE IN CONFORMATION: Balance in conformation is

achieved when the head, neck, forequarters, barrel and hindquarters look as if they all belong to the same horse. To be correctly proportioned, the horse should be symmetrical and smooth with a blending of all component parts, for this results in over-all balance, style and beauty.

SIZE AND WEIGHT: The size desired may vary to some degree to meet the preference of individual owners and for the purposes for which the horse is used. Historically the Quarter Horse of the West was a relatively low, small horse, for he lived on range forage with little or no supplement in his diet; his hard work on the feed that was available helped him develop some of his most outstanding characteristics: hardy, tough, thrifty. An over-large horse is likely to lose his surefootedness, soundness and nimbleness, all invaluable characteristics of the all-around Quarter Horse.

There may be some variation of bone size, for the large horse obviously needs more bone than the small one. Many horsemen prefer a middle-ground assessment of bone structure, realizing that the extra large bone is not necessarily the strongest bone, and may, in some instances, reflect the influence of work stock blood. The light-boned horse, excepting the deer-legged, is often somewhat more nimble footed and places the feet deftly in rough terrain and with less chance to become unsound. Many horsemen believe a medium sized flat bone is the most suitable for horses assigned to general use.

The generally accepted height and weight limits for mature Quarter Horse mares and stallions is 14.3 to 15.1 hands, 1,100 to 1,300 pounds.

11
Why Geldings?

Not so long ago I was working as a committee member on one of the West's top Quarter Horse shows. At our initial meeting, several months before the show was slated, the subject of geldings and gelding classes was discussed. One of our members spoke up against the conformation class for geldings.

"Why geldings?" he asked. "Why a class for animals that can't reproduce their own likeness? Why this in a breed show where stallions and mares are judged on good traits of conformation that they are likely to pass on when they are bred?"

We let him talk, allowing him to make his point, and then we all jumped on him at once. When we were through with him, he was an avid gelding fan.

We explained that the good Quarter Horse gelding is one of the breed's best advertisements. We offered him old programs from other shows, explaining that gelding classes have become so popular that in many instances these classes have more entries than any others. And we called his attention to the well-known fact that the gelding is the backbone of general all-around Quarter Horse activity.

Our ace in the hole for his support of the proposed halter class was this: at every show where performance classes are emphasized—cutting, reining, roping, pole bending, and whatnot—quality working geldings will attend, thus stimulating an added interest in the halter class as well as in the performance classes in which these same horses are competing.

We held our gelding conformation class this year, as we will every year, and we had a corral full of darned good horseflesh entered in it.

Mac McHugh, celebrated West Coast trainer, spins a stout Quarter Horse that he is training.

There are thousands of people all over the country, and thousands of growing youngsters, who want horses. These people are not breeders or professional horsemen; they are just folks who want a good safe horse to ride. Nine times out of ten they want a gelding. It goes without saying that many more folks who are professional or working horsemen are also looking for good geldings.

Today they do not have to look far. The gelding has come into an era of popular acclaim, and more breeders are castrating animals that a dozen years ago would have remained stallions. There are more really first-class Quarter Horse stallions today than ever before, and so it follows that there are more really first-class geldings. Today, in the age of keen Quarter Horse specialization, a breeder just cannot afford to maintain a mediocre stallion. There are too many good ones competing for his stud fee. So the intelligent breeder casts a critical look at each crop of yearlings and sharpens his knife accordingly.

Geldings have always been used in the rodeo arena and on the cattle ranch. Years ago it did not make much difference what the horse looked like just as long as he could get his chores done and remain sound for the next day's work. This has always been the criterion for a working horse: action, not beauty.

But today, even though a lot of cowboys will not admit it in so many words, a good looking horse is wanted as well as a good performer—especially if a cowboy wants to enter his horse in doing contests at the horse shows. True, judges are supposed to judge on working ability, but I have always maintained that if two horses are tied in a judge's mind as to performance, the one showing the most flash and pizzazz will get the nod and the blue ribbon.

Not so much in the cattle cutting game, where mares have outworked both geldings and stallions, and where also a stud can develop the reputation of being both a worker and a breeder, but in other phases of show performance, like reining and roping, geldings have been proven the best.

One of the most beautiful sights in the world of horses, I believe, is the prerodeo or preroping contest hour, when all the contestants and their mounts, usually geldings, are walking around or just loafing in the arena. At a big professional show, where you can find the best in the country, the horses are really something to see. Decked out in low roping saddles, breast collars, and split-ear bridles, these horses show all the characteristics for which they have become famous. Most of all, because they are geldings, they show cool-headedness, never kicking up much of a fuss, and they also show dependability.

John Dalton of Cheyenne, Wyoming, ropes and bulldogs on Quarter Horse geldings.

John Scott, Montana rancher and steer roper, poses on the old horse, Gayler, that took him to many a speedy steer.

On the other hand, stallions and mares are not always dependable; the latter become particularly nervous and excitable during the estrous cycle. But a gelding, whose reproductive powers are no more—and we all know that this does not affect a horse's ability to work—can concentrate fully on what he is doing. Mares do not attract him and other geldings do not worry him. So when he makes long, speedy runs after calves, and puts on the brakes with collisionlike suddenness, he is doing what he has been trained to do: concentrating on a repetitive act and tending strictly to business.

The market for such horses and others of proven working performance is high. The sum of three thousand dollars is not out of the ordinary to pay for a good rope horse. Some have sold even higher. A few years ago, Dean Oliver, many times world's champion calf roper, bought the magnificent sorrel roping gelding, Vernon, for five thousand dollars. Well-trained cutting horse geldings have sold for more than this.

If a man has a proven gelding that is winning consistently in performance contests, he can almost name his own price. And even young geldings, showing future ability as prospective roping, cutting, or reining horses, bring higher prices today than ever before.

Geldings are a tremendous advertising potential both for the ranch where they are bred and for the stallion that sires them. If a man sees a top-flight gelding at work, tries to buy him and cannot, he will usually inquire about his breeding and where he came from. If he figures that like begets like (and this is a popular modern-day breeding axiom), he will try his darndest to locate one of the same breeding.

Good sound ranch geldings, ready for anything when you want them to be ready, while perhaps not so handsome as their show brethren, are worth much money to the rancher who mounts several cowboys for roundup or simply for everyday ranch work. In good shape, well fed but not too fat, a gelding is a hard-working animal; he can usually take more than his rider can hand out. Nothing will ever replace the many different jobs of the horse on a big cow and calf ranch.

And when it comes to children in the saddle, I would rather have my kids on the back of a gentle gelding than on a pony or a burro.

A friend of mine once bought a five-year-old gelding to rope on. A good rope horse, the gelding was full of go in the arena. In fact, he was a little bit too high. Outside the arena, he was as gentle as a big family dog, and all the neighborhood kids, including my friend's own children, rode him. One day, shortly after this friend acquired the gelding, we had him saddled up ready to go to a jackpot roping. He was tied to the corral fence and we were inside eating an early lunch.

The late Walt Coburn, well-known western writer, loved Quarter Horses and rode them many an hour for pure relaxation.

When we stepped outside, the horse's new owner froze in his tracks. His four-year-old daughter had dragged an old chair up beside the horse, stepped up on it, grabbed the saddle strings and was literally pulling herself into the saddle. It gave us quite a start at first, but the gentle gelding never moved a muscle throughout the whole operation.

The ideal gelding, like any horse that a man uses, should be dependable, alert, athletic, balanced in movement, with a good disposition, and should look, to the eye of the beholder, like his kind of horse.

12
Trailering Your Quarter Horse

Quarter Horse people have always been the do-it-yourself kind, and proof of this statement is the fact that many of these horsemen haul their own horses with their own cars and trailers. They haul them to rodeos, horse shows, polo matches, cutting contests, race meets, county and state fairs, sheriff's posse events, gymkhanas, and all sorts of riding club get-togethers.

Trailering is easy but there is more to it than simply buying a trailer, slapping a hitch on the back of your car, hooking up, shoving your horse into the stall, and taking off at a mile a minute for the closest pumpkin-rollin'. For those of you who may be new at the business of horse hauling, or for those folks planning to buy a trailer, here is some advice:

There is nothing mysterious or dangerous about pulling one or two horses behind your car in a one- or two-horse trailer. But some folks are apt to feel a little panicky the first time they get behind the wheel of a car that is dragging a horse in a trailer—especially when the horse bumps the tailgate or shifts his position and this new and sudden distribution of weight can be felt all through the car.

The best rule of the road, just as in driving a car without a trailer, is common sense. If you use common sense, you have already licked the few problems that confront you when you first haul a horse.

For instance, it comes naturally to the good driver to obey all traffic and speed signals, and if in doubt to slow down. Even with power brakes, there is a tremendous amount of weight to keep under control as you slow your car down. There is no telling when you will have to execute an emergency stop. Most of the time if you drive in such a way that sudden, last-moment stops are unnecessary, you will be safer

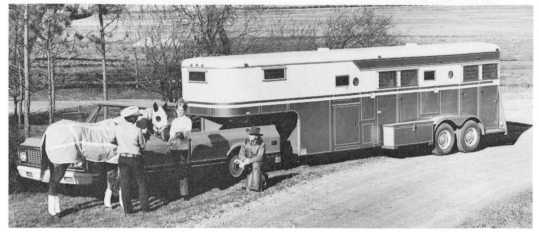

This very elaborate horse trailering van by Miley Trailer Company of Fort Worth is the ultimate in luxury but can still be hooked to the ranch pick-up. *Courtesy Darol Dickinson.*

and much kinder to your horse than if you are forever pounding on the brake pedal with your foot.

In taking sharp turns, too, you must slow down more than you normally would without a trailer behind you. The precaution is two-fold: it is safer on your whole rig and your horse will suffer less chance of being thrown off balance if you ease him around curves.

One of the most important parts of all trailering is loading. And here again common sense and a regard for the age and temperament of the horses you are loading pay off in big dividends.

Most aged horses that have been hauled before are usually good loaders. They willingly enter a trailer stall and stand quietly without any trouble. With green horses or young colts, a few problems may arise. You have to show patience with such stock and try to make them understand that there is nothing to fear. When loading green stock, pick an area clear of machinery and junk, so if your horse does throw a wingding he will not hurt himself.

Many farms and ranches build permanent installations for loading horses into trailers. Most of these are box- or chute-shaped. Dirt can be thrown in between two sides of heavy bolted lumber. It should be packed down hard and solid until the "floor" stands up ten or twelve inches. One end should slope to ground level. The other should butt up against and be level with the floor of the trailer.

When young horses are walked into this loading chute, a bar is positioned behind them or a gate is closed. There is no place for them to go except into the open end of the trailer. They cannot hurt themselves in such an enclosure and after some gentle persuasion soon learn to walk right into the trailer stall.

The interior of a trailer should be checked thoroughly from time to time for breaks, cracks, sharp edges—anything that might harm a horse. And it is a darned good idea to pay particular heed to the floors of old trailers. A new floor when needed is cheaper than a good horse with a broken leg. The inside of a trailer should be well padded and the floor should be covered with a tough, rubber, safety tread matting to assure good footing.

Most horsemen put a good deal of attention into the front of their trailers. Obviously the hitches should be strong—on both car and trailer end—and the connections or couplings should also be as strong as possible. There are several different kinds of lock connections, but the most popular is the ball hitch with the Bulldog snap.

Many horsemen like large Plexiglas windows on trailer fronts, enabling drivers to see right through the trailer with a turn of the head

Horse trailers come in various sizes and colors. Here is another nice one from the Miley people.

Trailers like these still get the job done for their owners in some of the more isolated livestock communities of the Southwest.

or a glance in the rear-view mirror. These big, roomy windows—sometimes just one—allow a horse to see ahead and ride with more ease. Horses actually learn to brace in a trailer against the turns, and if they can see the turns coming up, they are just that much more prepared. Topless trailers are almost a thing of the past, but if you happen to have one, Plexiglas goggles will protect your horse's eyes from wind and airborne particles.

You must have lights on the back of your trailer. State laws require that a double-horse trailer be equipped with twin taillights. Safety chains to be used in addition to the hitch coupling are also mandatory. Reflectors on the tailgate help other cars to spot you on the road, and reflecting tape can be used in attractive designs—initials or brands—on the back.

When hauling a long way, you should plan your trip ahead of time so you will know where and when you are stopping overnight. All horsemen have a lot in common, and in the fraternity of horse lovers, almost any one of them will gladly provide feed and water and a stall for a visiting horse. So let your buddies know you are coming their way. Even strangers are mighty friendly to traveling horsemen.

In hot weather, you can water your horses in the trailer when you stop for gas, and a little hay scattered in the feed troughs now and then keeps horses pretty contented.

The middle partition in a trailer, dividing the space of a double trailer into two separate stalls, should not be too far off the ground. If it is, and you happen to be hauling young stock, a colt may catch a leg under it and sustain a severe injury if not a broken bone.

And speaking of injuries to foals, many can be avoided by loading a mare and her foal into separate stalls, leaving the partition in between. A fast emergency turn of the wheel can send a mare reeling against her foal. Separate housing can protect them both. The foal should be tied up as well as the mare. Stop every three to four hours and let the foal nurse the mother.

Tail bandages and leg bandages should be used according to the habits of the horses being hauled. A horse that rides the tailgate continually should have his tail bandaged near the root. Likewise, a horse that is always stepping on or cutting his own legs should wear leg wraps.

Blanket horses in cold weather; allow for all possible ventilation in hot weather, but prevent hot, gusty winds from blowing directly into a horse's face.

You will learn all these things and probably lots more—relative to your particular situation—when you start taking your own horses to the shows. It is a do-it-yourself chore that is both fun and practical. Just remember those extra thousands of pounds that will affect your driving when starting, turning, and stopping.

13
Art and the Quarter Horse

For centuries the horse has been glorified through paintings and statues. Mighty generals and superb athletes, plus entire racial cultures like some American Indian tribes, have been preserved in horse art. The settling of the American West, which produced the cowboy, the cow horse, and vast herds of cattle, gave such men as Charlie Russell, Frederic Remington, Will James, and Edward Borein, probably the four greatest artists of the early days, a fantastic range of subject matter. Portrayal of the American West, including its men and horses, is still a challenge to painters and sculptors, because such canvases and bronzes are still in demand by collectors and, no doubt, always will be.

Two fine artists that I knew and liked were the late Hughlette "Tex" Wheeler, whose home was Florida, and the late George Phippen, whose home was Arizona. They loved horses of all kinds but were mostly attracted to the western horse—the Quarter Horse.

Tex Wheeler worked on the theory that a horse, like a human, had individual character. No two live horses, he told himself, ever looked exactly alike. Therefore, no two bronze horses should ever look exactly alike. To get the fine, accurate detail that Tex was so particular about, most of his models were cast by the lost wax process in which, in the last operation, a wax image of the statue is melted out of a fireproof cast and then molten bronze is poured into the cavity.

His works were not well known in the sense that they were universally popular or "best sellers." Tex led a quiet, unassuming life, and his work was not artistically or commercially well known to the general public. But to a small group of amateur and professional horsemen, scattered on both sides of the United States, he was the best

The mule-footed Quarter racing mare, Queenie, was perfectly captured in bronze by Tex Wheeler.

there was in his field, and his passing left a void that will never be filled in precisely the same way.

Tex was a genius. Even though his bronze models were sometimes unfavorably criticized by art "experts," they were more often praised by the persons for whom he was working. "After all," Tex used to say, "I'm doing this stuff for horsemen—not critics!"

And the stuff he did for horsemen, in its own way, was just as great as the stuff Remington, Russell, and James did for the Old West. These men were authentic and because of this trait they will live forever in the minds of the people who appreciate authentic art. Tex Wheeler, too, was authentic. It was impossible for him to be anything else. When he set out to reproduce an animal, he reproduced a perfect replica of the subject.

He cared little for formal art criticism, good or bad. On the other hand, he valued highly the opinions of his friends who owned, rode, or bred horses. And his friends' viewpoints occasionally changed the minds of the critics.

A polo bronze was once so maligned by some so-called art experts that Tex began to doubt his own ability. The piece under fire was

Another Wheeler. An Arizona cowboy, with chaps and tapaderos, mounted on a Quarter Horse cow pony.

called *Tail Shot*, an intricate portrayal of a very difficult off-side back shot under the tail of the player's pony. Tex liked the piece. He had spent many hours of hard work on it. But the more he listened to the critics, the more skeptical of it he became.

"Impossible!" the critics objected. "An utterly impossible shot!" They were convinced that the artist knew absolutely nothing about polo or horses.

Finally Tex invited some of his buddies—in this case, all high-goal polo players—to give the art experts a talk on *Tail Shot*. And when the discussion was over, after the critics had been briefed on what a tail shot was and how it was executed, there was a sudden about-face movement in the enemy's camp. *"Tail Shot,"* said one expert who had originally lambasted the statue, "is a unique demonstration of sheer virtuosity in solving the complex problem of balance and jet-propelled action."

Two of his very close friends, who helped materially to further his career and who probably knew Tex better than anyone else, were Rukin Jelks and Melville Haskell, both of Tucson, Arizona.

Jelks, a racer of Quarter Horses and Thoroughbreds, in whose stable through the years were such notables as Piggin String, Queenie, Red Skin, Miss Todd, and Old Pueblo, once told me this about Tex: "I haven't seen any other artist who could do a portrait of a horse and do it so realistically. Tex could shape up a horse's personality perfectly after the first rough draft in clay."

Haskell, who also raised Thoroughbreds and Quarter Horses and who is generally credited with devising the rules and regulations of modern-day short horse racing, told me recently: "Without reservation

A mother protects her foal. In this bronze can be seen the fine detail for which Tex Wheeler was so well known.

A close friend of the author's, the late George Phippen, was doing some wonderful bronzes and drawings before his untimely death.

he was great and he got great likenesses. He had the extraordinary talent of catching the perfect likeness of an animal."

The childhood ambition of George Albert Phippen was to become an artist. On his father's farm in Kansas, when just a little toddler, George spent late afternoons modeling crude clay figures on the banks of a stream, dreaming that someday he could do this sort of thing—and draw, too—all day long.

What Phippen painted came out of the man himself. He hardly ever used models and he never copied from photographs or other art. He had great powers of observation and a memory like a sponge. He was a tireless researcher, and his preparatory trips took him to libraries, museums, old houses in the back country, ranches, farms, or to the tops of mountain peaks.

Like Tex Wheeler, authenticity is what he strove for more than anything else. A friend once told him that he thought the key to Russell's success was authentic portrayal and razor-sharp action. Phippen always remembered that and never started a drawing until, in his own mind, he felt every minute detail was worked out clearly and precisely.

He drew anything concerning the new and the old West, but his specialty was animal action, such as bucking horses, stampeding steers, or wild animals. In his pictures, he liked to create atmosphere and tell a story at the same time. In the tradition of Russell, he gave each drawing an appropriate name.

George was born in Charles City, Iowa, on July 11, 1915, the son of a horseman and farmer. When he was three years old, the family moved to another farm in Kansas, and George began his education a few years later in a little country schoolhouse near Emmett.

About this time he started modeling with clay and sketching with pencils. His father, who was also artistically talented, used to draw and then cut out horses and cattle and other animals on plain white paper for George and his brother.

"One day," George once told me, "I guess Dad got tired of doing this for us because he said, 'Here, you fellows are old enough to make your own livestock,' and he handed us the pencil and scissors. From that moment on we drew and cut out our own horses and cattle. The first were pretty hard looking. But I only wish I had a cow herd in the flesh as large as that paper herd got to be. It sure would take a lot of range to hold the fat on them. I even drew and scissored out cattle in school when I should have been studying. I got my ears boxed many times. One teacher used to make me stand by her desk and study so that she could keep her eye on me. Or sit at a front desk near her. I spent most of my time at these two places, and because of that, there was many a horse, steer, cowboy, and Indian that never got finished."

Few illustrators have ever captured the likeness of the Quarter Horse in the manner achieved by Phippen, which simply meant that George knew horses—Quarter Horse types—as well as he knew how to mix colors or daub a brush. I feel that Phippen was one of the first artists, if not *the* first, to give a little polish to the western cowboy's horse. He pictured them with short, glossy coats, with clipped manes, with well-shod hooves, with powerful muscling in the forearms and gaskins, and with perfectly balanced bodies. In other words, he discarded the Indian pony and the cowboy mustang of the old days (at least in his portrayal of the modern West) and used the well-groomed, breedy-looking Quarter Horse type as a model for most of his pictures. For this he will have the everlasting thanks of the Quarter Horse fraternity.

14
Roping Clubs and How to Organize Them

Roping running critters from horseback is such a popular pastime in the West today—and in other sections of the country, too—that I think there should be more roping clubs. However, there seems to be a dearth of such organizations, and many of those that I have seen have been poorly or haphazardly set up. Many towns and livestock communities have started roping clubs only to find, due to lack of money, interest, or participation, that they soon had a bad deal on their hands, a sort of here-today-gone-tomorrow association. In fact, the mortality rate of roping clubs is tremendous.

The purpose of this chapter is to outline, giving suggestions here and there, my idea of a successful, organized group of amateur ropers. But first, let's define *successful* as the word that will be used in this piece.

Successful is not going to mean financial gains in this case. It is next to impossible to make money from a roping club unless other considerations are brought into play. In this instance, successful will mean harmonious to all, with cooperation from all.

Any group of amateur ropers in a typical small community should found their club on a cooperative basis, excluding the idea of any one or two individuals making money off the others, with each member striving toward a smooth-running club. A new group should try to get as many initial members as possible, provided they are all fairly compatible and do not differ too widely in lariat skill and arena ideas. After the club gets going, then any number of lads can be allowed entry regardless of their talent and thoughts. By then the majority rule of fair play and decision should be well established for the mutual benefit of all members.

Roping clubs can be anywhere, fenced by any material—pipes, wire, or boards—and can have top ropers as members. The veteran Ted Powers in action here. *Courtesy Tommy Thompson.*

But first of all you have got to get a bunch of fellows together who like to rope and want to start a club. It might start while two boys sit hunkered in the shade at some riding stable or ranch bunkhouse.

"Why," asks one, "can't we start a club where we could rope as much as we want without having to bother old Charley all the time about bringing his calves in from the foothills and using his land and chutes?"

"Hey, now!" the other exclaims. "We could use that vacant five acres of Chuck's that he's always going to put in alfalfa but never does, and Jack can get a dozen or so calves from his old man."

"Yeah, and Joe's dad has a feed store and maybe we can get hay cheaper from him, and the Leonard brothers own a lumber yard and I know they'll help with fencing and with some chutes and pens."

This may sound idyllic and far too easy, but the point of the conversation is simply to impress upon the founders of future roping clubs that it is much simpler to make it a community project than for one or two men to try and do it all alone.

Stock, feed, lumber, and wire, and any other incidentals, should be obtained from those who have an interest, either direct or indirect, in the proceedings if possible. All expenses for building and for obtaining the calves, too, should be split among the founding members.

And speaking about the construction of fences and chutes: use the best. I have seen far too many cheap, dilapidated fences, chutes, and catch pens begin to fall apart after a year or so, putting an extra burden of expensive repairs on club members.

Any level plot of ground big enough for a horseman to handle calves in will do to fence. A fence of sturdy cedar posts and smooth wire, preferably five or six strands deep, is good. A still stouter fence to hold steers can be made of railroad ties and heavy mesh wire. Separate catch pens should be erected at both ends of the field out of the same durable materials, perhaps of double strength. When building any rodeo or roping field, build for permanency. A well-built field should, with occasional repairs, last a lifetime.

When you come to the chute and chute box, make the box a good, deep one, so that you can take a long run to score the calf. Another reason for the deep box: many fellows will be around with green horses to work and train. There is nothing better than a deep, roomy chute box to handle a young horse in when you are first running a few head on him.

You can also use a longer barrier when you have matched ropings and jackpots, and you will have plenty of them when things get rolling. It is my opinion that we all rope over too short a score nowadays. This is necessary in many rodeo arenas, but in practice we should take longer runs at the stock. It is better for the horses and it just feels better all around to have to "power" your way further to that fleet-legged junior Brahman.

Always keep the chute gate, as well as any gates to your arena, in good swinging order. See to it that the barrier cord and spring are always in good shape. If you plan a small timekeeper's box above the catch pens next to the chute—an unnecessary expense, but nice to park the little woman in when you are showing off—here are a few ideas for it: cover it from the sun; provide a sturdy ladder or stairs for entry; get a bench and a couple of wide boards to write on; keep a box, fastened to the floor, with such items as tools, first aid, a sharp knife, a rodeo rule book, and a ball of twine for second loop strings.

Now that the field and chutes are built and if your gang still has enough money to feed its horses, you can think about the calves. In case Jack's old man does not cotton to the idea of loaning out calves to be roped, you can pick up some, usually at a fair price, from local sales or small operators. While you are in the market for calves, keep your eye on magazine and newspaper livestock classifieds, too.

The day comes when you have got your calves and, since the arena

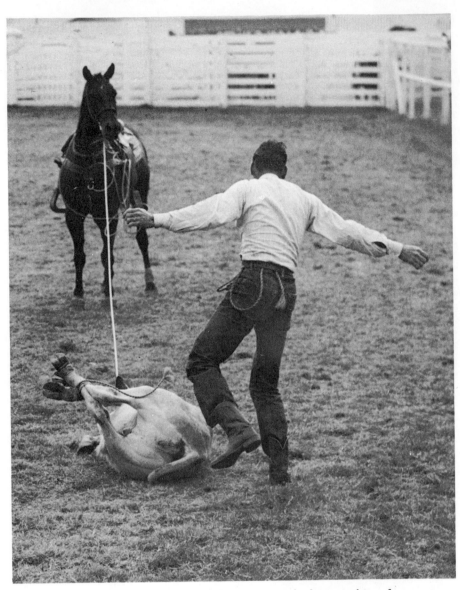

Fast time in a Colorado roping club arena might be anything from twenty to fourteen seconds. *Courtesy Lee Merrill and Associates.*

and chutes have been waiting for them, there is only one thing left to do—ROPE!

But now comes a problem. There were eight of you who started the club, and during the time you were getting organized and building and gathering stock, you recruited fifteen members at ten dollars a head (that helped a little on expenses). But three of these members, you soon discover, act as if they were born with a rope in their hands. Each Sunday, between them, they eat up all the dollar jackpot money with their 15 flats and 14.1s.

Some of the other fellows begin to gripe, so the charter members have to tackle the problem. Here is one way to counteract a roping flash among roping blurs, and even up a jackpot made up of unbalanced roping talent.

You hold your first jackpot and then handicap the fastest ropers and aid the slowest ones. This takes a bunch of arithmetic, but you knew that shade on the raised stand would come in handy for keeping the sun off some of the boys' best girls as they juggle your roping figures.

All the boys who roped under 15 seconds get four seconds added to their time for the next jackpot. Those between 15 and 20 seconds get two seconds added. All from 20 to 25 get two seconds subtracted from their next roping times; those above 25 seconds get four seconds subtracted.

In other words, if Buck ties in the first jackpot in 14.9 and in the second jackpot he ties in 17, his time in the second roping, with four seconds added, will be 21. If Joe ties in the first jackpot in 26.2 and in the second he wraps one up in 23, his corrected time in the second roping, with four seconds subtracted, will be 19.

Another way of trying to even up a bunch of amateurs, after you know your calves, is to let the fast boys rope the tough calves and to let the slower boys rope the "dead" ones. Still another way, if an even number of ropers contest, is to have two boys combined as a team. If there are twenty-four ropers, there will be only twelve times, the fastest total determining the winning twosome. Pairs of ropers can be selected, such as a fast boy and a slow boy, or names can be drawn from a hat.

If your club advances to the stage where it can sponsor team roping and you invest in twelve or fifteen steers, here is an excellent way to even the jackpots. Put all the heelers' names in one hat, the headers' names in another. Then let the headers draw from the hat holding the heelers and vice versa. It is possible that two experts will get together, but usually the division will be fair as to team handiness with ropes.

Arizonan Sam McKinney is shown on the famous gelding, Thistle, by Cowboy P-12. This gelding once sold for five thousand dollars. He was a great rope horse. *Courtesy Richard Schaus.*

The famous veteran roper and horse trainer, Jess Goodspeed, poses on Pistol's Hornet, former AQHA Calf Roping Champion of 1966 and owned by Roland Stacey of Natchez, Mississippi. *Courtesy Spencer Studio.*

This method works well at Willcox, Arizona's roping club where there are many crack combinations of team-tyers.

Jackpot ropings will generally be held only on Sunday. The calves should have a rest the day before, for three and four jackpots can be worked in on Sunday when all the members gather for their weekend recreation. Another rest for the calves on Monday, and during the middle of the week your club can hold practice sessions.

It is customary at most clubs to charge a slight fee per head, which goes for arena maintenance and animal fodder, when no jackpots are being held. Let's say the fee is two bits for members and fifty cents for nonmembers. By watching the boys rope throughout the week you can pretty well tell what kind of ropers they are, how they are mounted, and how they will be handicapped during the jackpots. There are a number of different handicapping methods, besides the ones mentioned, that can be worked out to the special needs of a club.

Here are some final suggestions for the lasting success of your club, which, in the long run, as I have emphasized, will depend on the support of its own members. Stimulate this support. Give a prize every month for the fastest calf tied, for the most improvement in horse and roper, and to the guy with the worst run of luck. Then every three months, give a more elaborate prize, a silver and gold buckle or something similar, to the roper who has roped and tied the fastest twenty-five head of calves.

Roping matches create much interest among ropers, and if there are any other clubs in neighboring towns, arrange a series of matches with the four or five top loop-dabbers from each outfit. And roping matches between your own members should also keep interest at a high pitch. And that is what you want. You want to keep your members happy and interested in roping.

15
Are Quarter Horse Families Important?

In the old days of the West, a man usually selected his horse for its individual conformation and ability. If the horse's ancestry was known, so much the better. But bloodlines and pedigrees were of secondary consideration—not because they were not important, but because they were often unavailable or fabricated.

Today it is a different story. As the Quarter Horse breed grows, becoming steadily more proficient in specialized activities, horsemen are becoming more interested in the background of their specialty mounts. Quarter Horse families are becoming increasingly more important.

What is a Quarter Horse family? How do we define it? What are the factors that make up a family?

I think the best way to answer these questions would be to take a particular breeding line and study it. And of all the Quarter Horse or Thoroughbred sires that have fathered a family line, none is more famous or well known than Peter McCue.

Peter McCue was a great individual horse, and I feel the argument that has raged in Quarter Horse circles about his breeding is senseless when we consider the many other fine Quarter Horse family sires that were of unknown or questionable ancestry. (The AQHA confirms that the horse was by Dan Tucker out of Nora M.)

He was foaled at Petersburg, Illinois, in 1895, and a few years later, when his first colts were dropped, the Peter McCue family was established. (Helen Michaelis, former AQHA secretary who made a prolonged study of the old horses, gives the date of 1899 for the establishment of the Peter McCue family.)

In the following years Peter McCue sired such wonderful old horses

Raising Quarter Horse foals from special bloodlines can be both fun and rewarding.

as Harmon Baker, Hickory Bill, Badger, Jack McCue, Chief, Sykes, and John Wilkens—and from these stallions came other great sires such as Dodger, Big Nigger, Paul Ell, Old Sorrel, Midnight, El Rey RO, and Joe Hancock.

So we begin to see that a truly great Quarter Horse family is one deriving from a single stallion, who begets sons who in turn become great sires themselves. And through this breeding process, which can continue on for generations, the qualities and characteristics of the original founding stallion are maintained faithfully—even perhaps improved on in certain sensational breeding nicks.

Still another requisite of an outstanding family line is the ability of sons or grandsons or great grandsons of the original sire to start their own line—a sort of family within a family. What Quarter Horse breeder has not heard of Old Sorrel, the foundation sire of the King Ranch Quarter Horses? Old Sorrel was a son of Hickory Bill and a grandson of Peter McCue.

What professional rodeo roper has not heard of Joe Hancock, the original sire of a line of rugged, active, and speedy calf and steer horses? He was by John Wilkens by Peter McCue, and he sired, among others, Red Man, Roan Hancock, Hancock King, and Joe Hancock, Jr. And these sons of old Joe in turn sired some of the best short-distance race horses and rodeo rope horses in the Southwest.

Joe Hancock, Jr., got Pelican, an extremely fast straightaway race horse; Roan Hancock got Roper and Dusty Hancock, both arena mounts and racers; and Red Man got Worryman, Wampus Kitty, and John Red, racehorses, and a whole barn full of arena horses, registered and unregistered.

Another sign of a great family line is when the male horses remain strong producers of the desired characteristics, even when crossed on different kinds of mares, some of which may be of inferior type. In the early 1900s there was much indiscriminate horse breeding, yet many of the top Quarter Horse families kept their distinguishing character-istics despite breeding experiments and abuses. Joe Hancock's mother, for instance, was a half-Percheron mare, yet old Joe retained the tre-mendous speed of his sire, John Wilkens, and, as I have pointed out, went on to become a splendid sire in his own right.

But indiscriminate matings of horses for the most part are a thing of the past. Now all sorts of records, pedigrees, and statistics are proc-essed by the AQHA and its Racing Division and are readily available to the serious horseman. And the demand for such material—extended pedigrees, stud books, stallion information, and performance records—proves that Quarter Horse families are very important to modern breeders.

Speed is the basic ingredient of any worthwhile horse. If a good horse has speed to begin with, then he can be trained for almost anything. But speed alone is something that you cannot put in a horse if he has not already got it. And that is why in the most extended Quarter Horse pedigrees we find Thoroughbred blood cropping up here and there.

The Leamington line is a family of terrifically fast blood. Leamington was an imported Thoroughbred stud who sired Enquirer who sired Faustus who sired Bonnie Joe who sired Joe Blair who sired Joe Reed who sired Joe Reed II. And Joe Reed II was the father of Bull's Eye, Lady Gray, Rusty, Hy Myrt, Little Sister W., Whisper W., and the great Leo, one of the outstanding sires of Quarter Running Horses.

The Himyar (TB) line is another one that should be of particular interest to Quarter Horse men. One of the great, great great grandsons

Red Man, who was by Joe Hancock by John Wilkens by Peter McCue, was a top sire of rope horses. His ears were frozen off in Montana when he was a colt.

of Himyar was Question Mark, who sired My Question, Osage Red, Gray Question, and Savannah G. Another fifth generation descendant of Himyar was Beggar Boy, a Thoroughbred that left his mark in Oklahoma on both racehorses and rope horses. By Black Toney, Beggar Boy fathered Blackout, Baldy Boy, and Buster, a great all-around rope horse who was owned by Ike Rude. (Black Gold, a full brother to Beggar Boy, won the Kentucky Derby in 1924, beating 19 starters on a fast mile-and-a-quarter track in a time of 2:05 1/5.)

The Bend Or family is another good one that has been responsible for many running horses and Oklahoma Star, one of the greatest rope horse sires in the history of rodeo. Oklahoma Star was by Dennis Reed by Lobos by Golden Garter (imported) by Bend Or—all Thoroughbreds—yet old Star sired Nickels, one of the best Sooner State steer horses, and Croppie, a Jess Goodspeed calf horse about whom Jess said: "He was the best calf horse I ever roped on."

Of course there are many other families, both Quarter Horse and

Jay and Polly Parsons, ranchers from Cody, Wyoming, enjoy raising Quarter Horses that are athletes in every equine sense. Shown is the mare Linda Mujer.

Thoroughbred, to be considered in breeding programs. One of the best for pure Quarter Horse bloodlines was in the Traveler (himself of unknown breeding) family. King, Jess Hankin's splendid stud, was by Zantanon by Little Joe by Traveler. And King sired Poco Bueno, a stallion who transmitted exceptional conformation to his get.

So no matter what a man is looking for—speed, action, disposition, conformation, bottom, anything—family bloodlines are important to study. For within family lines we can find the characteristics we want. We can probe back to see how consistently these characteristics have been bred down, generation by generation, and we can select our own breeding stock or individual using horses accordingly.

16
The Quarter Horse as a Cow Pony

The late Billy Anson, Quarter Horse breeder and cattleman of west Texas, years ago once said, "The Quarter Horse does not fear the advent of the automobile." Dan Casement, writing the introduction for the first AQHA Stud Book and Registry in 1941, confirmed Anson's statement by saying, "How right he was is attested by the now well recognized fact that the Quarter Horse has no equal in working cattle, the one and only field of equine activity wherein horses are destined *never* to slump in positive economic value."

On all the big cattle ranches in this country today, and on the small ones, too, the cow herds and beef steers are worked in the main by Quarter Horses. Many very large outfits, like the King Ranch in Texas, raise their own horses for their own ranch use.

From its famous foundation sire, Old Sorrel by Hickory Bill by Peter McCue, the King Ranch developed a superior family of Quarter Horses all sorrel in color. These Quarter Horses, although they could also run a lick, were produced for cow horses. It has been said that the culling of the brood mare band was sometimes pretty ruthless. Only the very best were kept as brood matrons to breed to sons and grandsons of Old Sorrel.

Ask any real cowboy what is the most important part of his job and he will say, "Why that's easy enough to answer—my pony, for sure!" His pony, for sure, would be the right answer, too. Along about here some mechanized cowpoke is apt to pipe up to cite the ability of the Jeep or the pick-up or the half-ton truck, implying that perhaps, after all, the horse has seen his day. But, I repeat, the real cowboy's answer is one hundred percent correct. The cow pony is, and will continue to

This buckskin cow horse, probably a Quarter Horse, goes about his chore of pulling a Hereford calf to a hot branding iron on a Texas Panhandle ranch.

be, the one most important element in the life of the working cowboy.

Now before I go any further, I am going to give a very simple definition of what I consider a working cowboy to be: he is a man (or boy) who works with cows (or steers, or bulls, or calves) on a cattle ranch. My definition of a cattle ranch is a spread of land—and for illustrative purposes, let's make it a big spread—whose owner or owners breed and raise beef cattle for a livelihood.

My definition of a cow horse is a horse that is ridden by this kind of a cowboy on this kind of a spread.

In the old days working cow horses were really *working* cow horses, for there was not much play and horse shows and rodeos were as scarce as pearl-snap buttons. The horses and riders kept pretty much on the job. When they were not working, they relaxed and rested up for more work.

With horse shows and rodeos nowadays as common as fancy shirts, we are apt to confuse the working cow horse with the many-performance show horses exhibited from Canada to Mexico and from Florida to California. These are not what we call working cow horses; they are show horses, specialty horses. This classification is not intended to be derogatory, for most of these animals are fine horses, worth much money in their respective specialty fields. For instance, top cutting horses that win a lot of *dinero* for their owners each year are not worked excessively hard on most big spreads. These spreads have other horses for their cowboys, not specialty horses, and it is these horses we are interested in.

Several years ago at a Texas horse show, a horseman nudged me and said, "Now there's a pretty class of horses for you, but I wonder if they can do anything. You know," he continued, "these Quarter Horse shows are like bathing beauty contests; they line all the good looking ones up in bathing suits, but it takes the ugly ones to really swim."

My first experience with real cow horses was in 1936 on the Cross Triangle Ranch north of Prescott, Arizona. I was just an awkward kid then, probably more in the way than helpful, but I will never forget the woolly times working my first cattle—and cattle horses.

Several of us were working the hill country back of the ranch headquarters, trying to flush a herd of wild white-faced cattle that had been running loose and inbreeding for years. On orders from the boss each summer, the cowboys had tried to clear out these animals and work them into open, flat country where they could be spotted and handled more easily. But it was a thankless, wearisome task that never seemed to get quite done, and the cattle left up there became wilder and wilder.

As anyone who has ever fooled with them knows, there is nothing quite so rank and snorty as a wild, mature cow, of any breed, with a wild, young calf at her side. It takes a heap of horse to overtake such an animal in that kind of country, rocky and rough with a thick blanket of cedar scrub covering the slopes and rises.

It is quite a thrill to come up over a rise and spot an old cow and her calf. The very second she gets wind of you or sees you, she spooks. And while she knows the country, you do not. But off you go after her, trying to head her toward the drift the boys built the winter before. If you can get her going along this fence, the battle will be half over, for she will eventually run into the big trap seven or eight miles down the fence.

But where is the cow now? Gone—off through the brush like a jack-rabbit, so you pull your pony up and try to find her tracks. You hear her on that next hill and spur your pony over the rocks. Then you tag her again and get her going in the right direction. After she's headed down, several other fellows along the fence keep her drifting along.

Not much of a hand at roping in those days, I just watched—if I could keep up with them—the other fellows rope the big wild steers that just would not be pushed down that drift fence. When a steer like this started to run, only the fastest of horses could catch it. Some chases lasted more than thirty minutes, but the strong, stout-hearted, sure-footed cow horse usually brought the cowboy up close enough for a throw.

If he was alone he was obliged to bust the steer; if he had a partner, they heeled and headed the steer and tied it to a tree until it was docile enough to be herded down the line.

For the most part that summer I rode a chute-crazy, former bull-dogging horse, one of twenty-five head of the Cross Triangle cow horse band. He was probably the sorriest horse of the bunch, but then I was

Pete Phelps, manager of the Santa Margarita Ranch near Sasabe, Arizona, works white-faced calves on his favorite Quarter Horse, Shotgun.

The cow horse is still used on all sorts of cattle spreads, despite Jeeps, trucks, and pick-ups.

Arizona rancher Manerd Gayler, mounted on a good ranch horse, looks over a herd of Texas Longhorns that he once ran for western movies.

probably the sorriest hand, too, so both of us made a good combination and learned together.

There are still plenty of places in the West that have enough land and enough cattle to warrant full-scale roundups with culling and cutting and branding and dehorning and castrating and driving and holding. On the roundups the ranch cutting horse really shines. Unlike the confined work of his brethren in the show ring, his job is apt to take him over many miles of terrain at high speeds.

In the show arena action is desired and stimulated on the part of the animal being cut out, but no such wild doings are wanted on the ranch. The quieter the job can be done, the better. But outlaw steers or prankish calves sometimes pop up in the most well-mannered herds, and when they do, the intelligence and nimbleness of the cutting horse is put to the test. The resulting action is ten times more exciting to watch than that of the show ring.

Of all cow horses, I most admire the rope horse—not the rodeo rope horse or any horse that simply pounds after a calf, puts on a tremendous stop, and backs up like lightning. These horses, like other professional arena horses, are highly trained and specialized and not what I call all-around ranch rope horses.

Real all-around ranch rope horses are inclined to be a little droopy and unexcitable. Theirs is a rather monotonous life: in a corral all day, heeling calves; out in the open, dragging calves to a branding iron; or catching and holding down heavier stuff for doctoring or marking. Any of these chores come as run-of-the-day events to the seasoned rope horses. Once they learn their duties, they execute them serenely, never expending an extra calorie if they can help it.

I have seen horses holding down big stock, pulling on the rope so hard it appeared that they were straining every muscle in their bodies. However, closer inspection showed that they were actually relaxed, merely leaning on the rope and wisely using their own weight as an anchor.

One of the worthiest characteristics of the cow horse is his disposition. We all know he is endowed with heart, courage, sagacity, and stamina, but his disposition and tractability are what give his rider faith in him. That even temperament is what allows the rider to anticipate almost every move and what lets the rider sit comfortably and easily in the saddle while the cow horse jogs along a section fence or over a mountain pass. This great hereditary trait also makes the cow horse beloved of ranch kids, too, for he can take almost anything the kids can dish out.

Gone are the days that Charlie Russell depicted in his wonderful painting called *A Bronc for Breakfast,* showing a waddie topping a full-bucking bronc precariously near the chuck wagon. Many old-timers may be saddened by the thought that perhaps in the next fifty years or so, the buck will be gone from all horses. This idea is not too far-fetched. If it ever should come true, I do not think the result will be so bad. I believe the spirit and zip of our Quarter Horse cow ponies will still be there, all right, but it will be directed and controlled into a useful channel. The buck is going out of our cow horses, but the "cow" is still there and always will be.

17
Cutting Horses Past and Present

Booted gents in the West have discovered that the cutting horse knows more tricks than a boomtown dance-hall girl on Saturday night. They learned this soon after the National Cutting Horse Association was founded at Fort Worth, Texas, in 1946. They learned how to train a cutting horse prospect and they learned how to ride and show a cutting horse, until today cattle carving contests at horse shows and rodeos are filled with swifter movement and fancier action than were ever seen on the rangeland in past years.

This is not to say that the old-time cutting horse was a slowpoke. As I have pointed out, his primary function on the range was and is to get the job done with a minimum of fuss. But his arena counterpart is admittedly a flashier performer.

The cutting horse, past and present, is a combination of speed, alertness, intelligence, and ready-wittedness. He carries no particular type of conformation, his coat can be any color, and his blood need not stem from any one kind of breed. He can be hot- or cold-blooded and can look, as cowboys say, "like a dawg." With the cutting horse, beauty takes a back seat. (However, in the show arena, it is a different story: it is estimated that over ninety-two percent of all cutting horses that appear in professional shows are registered Quarter Horses, just another proof of the amazing ability of the Quarter Horse.)

Around the years after 1860 there were an estimated 3,500,000 head of cattle in Texas and its adjoining borders. Many of the cattle were in a half-wild condition, roaming free over much of the land. In the fall and spring, ranchers gathered together for their semi-annual roundups, at which time the animals, according to different markings and brands,

Senor George, with Sonny Perry up, was the NCHA's champion cutter for the year 1961.

would be herded together and culled for additional branding, marketing, doctoring, and anything else the stock owners wanted to do with them. Many thousands of head of Longhorns were handled as a single unit. For miles around the cowboys would drive their own stock and the stock of others to a "holding ground" or "home station." Here the separating or cutting would begin.

Here, also, is where the cutting horse first won his spurs. Into the herd he would go—neck out, head low, ears pointed, eyes alert—to make his first cut. Nimble-hoofed, he would ease through the milling animals, held by the encircling wranglers, until he was sure of that animal which his rider selected to remove from the herd. Then he would slowly move the steer out to the edge of the herd and isolate it from the rest. When several animals of similar brands were bunched up away from the main herd, this new group was called the cut. As the work continued many more cuts of like brands would appear until the original mass of cattle was reduced to many smaller herds.

The late Frank W. Jordan, who once owned the Oatman Flat Ranch in the Gila River Valley district of Arizona, recalled huge herds of cattle of up to ten thousand head years ago in Texas around his father's outfit on the headwaters of Silver Creek, some fifteen miles south of Colorado City. Jordan remembered a cutting horse that was justly famous in Texas around 1884. He was just a kid when his father, Thomas A. Jordan, bought the horse from Jake Sykes, a prominent cattleman at the time.

They called the horse Jake after his former owner. He was a dun with a jet-black mane and tail. Although Sykes could not be sure, he thought Jake was of mustang heritage. Along the crown of his neck, about ten inches back of the ears, there was a definite scar as if he had been shot. In those days it was not uncommon for an expert marksman to hide out near the waterhole of a wild mustang bunch

In the early days of the NCHA, these five mounts—perhaps the greatest five cutting horses ever photographed together—won the rich show at San Antonio, Texas. They are from left to right: Caesar's Pistol, ridden by Jim Calhoun; Poco Bueno, ridden by Andy Hensley; Poco Tivio, ridden by Milt Bennett; Skeeter, ridden by Phil Williams; and Jesse James, ridden by Matlock Rose. *Courtesy Zintgraff Photographs.*

and crease a likely looking saddle prospect with a bullet. The shot would be just close enough to paralyze the horse temporarily.

But if Jake had been an outlaw, he certainly showed no signs of his wild past when Jordan got him. He was a five-year-old, with a wonderfully calm disposition and kind, gentle eyes. Fast and quick-moving, he stood fifteen hands and weighed close to eleven hundred pounds. He was well broken and already a made horse. Old Tom Jordan used him solely as a cutting horse, and his fame spread throughout the Lone Star State.

"In western Texas," Frank Jordan said, "there were few horsemen who didn't want to buy Jake. My father was offered as high as five hundred dollars for him, an awful lot of money for horseflesh in those times. But he never sold him and never let anybody else but my older brother cut cattle on him. Those two were the only men who ever worked Jake and he got the job done for them.

"I never once saw a steer or cow duck back on Jake. He was the greatest cutting horse I've ever seen and I think he was the greatest in Texas at that time. On the very edge of the herd where lots of stock is apt to duck back, Jake would work very slow and take his time, watching every quiver of the steer or cow ahead of him. Nothing ever bothered him. If an old cow tried to dodge around Jake on the edge of the herd, he would stand up and pivot from side to side on his hind legs, blocking her way at every turn. When he got tired of this, he'd give a big lunge and snap some of the hide off her back. Once she started to the cut, she went.

"In the summer of 1885," Frank Jordan went on, "after two years of severe cold and drought, the ranges of western Texas were way overstocked. Several outfits, including ours, pooled their herds and drove them to the Bear River country in New Mexico. My father left about two thousand head of cattle there and two hundred horses. Jake was one of them.

"We then came into Arizona territory and settled near Phoenix. In 1887 some of my family went back to the Bear River country and gathered up two hundred head of the fattest cattle and some fifty horses. You can bet Jake came along.

"We bought the Oatman Flat in 1890. Jake hadn't done any work to speak of in five years, but he never forgot he was a cutting horse. I remember once my brother was driving a few head of gentle milk cows up from pasture. One of the cows suddenly cut back along the fence. My brother was sitting relaxed in the saddle and not paying much attention to what was going on. Jake saw the cow, though, and

A characteristic of cattle-cutting Quarter Horses is to plaster their ears back, concentrating fully on keeping up with white-faced heifers. Here, a heifer turns out instead of in.

as fast as lightning he made a move to head her. He jumped so fast he moved right out from under my brother and left him sitting for a second where there was nothing at all to sit on."

Nowadays the huge cattle drives and immense roundups are a part of the past, but the cutting horse, whether he still works on the range or performs in the arena, does fundamentally the same thing he did years ago. He is strictly a working horse whose job it is to cut cattle under any and all types of conditions. Two main characteristics make a mount suitable for this purpose: an inherent cow sense, which enables the horse to outthink a spooky steer, and the physical aptitude to muster a burst of action, which also enables him to outmaneuver the steer.

A cutting horse can be compared to an ambidextrous athlete. Such a horse always has his wits about him and his legs well under him, and he can turn like a cat on either lead. Some horses, like left-handed or right-handed athletes, favor either a left or right turn. Not so the

Top cattle-carving horses are able to block every move of a cow brute.

cutting horse. He can stop, back up, lunge forward, and twist or turn in either direction with equal grace and coordination. His leads are always timely and correct so that he never gets tangled up or stumbles, unless his rider is at fault.

Occasionally you will see a horse working in a contest or on the ranch without a bridle. There is no particular advantage in this other than showing a horse off and demonstrating to a prospective buyer or audience that the horse is "plumb gentle and broke" to cutting cows. It is staunchly maintained by some old-time cattlemen that a horse used to a bridle and then trained a few times to work without one will soon do the job better with his head free of steel and leather. "He's not hampered," they insist, "by a riggin' over his head, and you don't want to use the reins anyway when you're carvin' stock out. To boot, the durn old fool knows he's free as the breeze and likes to strut his stuff and show off."

There is no denying that many cutting horses are braggarts, whether they work with a bit and headstall or without one. The horse somehow seems to know that his job is done with great skill and poise and that we humans think he is a pretty good type of equine. Watch him strut and swagger after pushing a fleet-legged steer all over the arena, or on the range after he has successfully driven a stubborn cow brute to the cut. He's proud of himself and he knows his rider is proud of him, though the cowboy may be so used to the procedure that he shows no emotion.

Some cutting horses have been trained to an almost unbelievable degree of proficiency. Take Powder Horn, for instance, the great steer-roping horse of the late Bob Crosby. Powder Horn, a big sorrel standing 15.3 and weighing 1,250 pounds, was not only a fine steer horse, but he had been trained to cut stock just as well as he busted heavy steers. Crosby put up Powder Horn open to the world for a five-thousand-dollar matched cutting contest. The horse would cut out almost anything that moved—goats, dogs, children, and even chickens. In exhibition, Crosby and Powder Horn used to cut chickens into a small box in the center of an arena. Crosby roped a steer on the horse once without a bridle, and thought nothing of cutting fifty or sixty head of cattle on Powder Horn while the horse was bareheaded.

A more recent talented cattle cutter—the 1971 NCHA World Champion Cutting Horse Mare—was Gandy's Time, owned by Jim Lee of Iowa Park, Texas. Early in 1972 she suffered a severe break of a foreleg attempting to escape from a tornado that hit the ranch. At the time of her death, she was ahead in NCHA standings for the 1972 championship.

Most men who train cutting horses say that very few individuals make top horses. It takes at least three years and sometimes six to eight years to put that necessary polish on a horse so that he knows what he is doing at all times, under any conditions. A small percentage of good cow horses make good cutting horses, but if a horse does show an abundance of cow sense at an early age, he will make a cutting horse much more quickly than one who does not. At two or three years, the prospective cutter should be taught what a cow is and be allowed to work with small herds. He should never be hurried or crowded, however, and when he is five or six he will know something about his work. From then on until an eight-year-old, he can be opened up in any way, forced and worked hard. If he is one in a hundred, then, from eight years of age until he is too old to twist and turn, he will carry his rider to top winnings at almost any big show and be a ranch horse of exceptional ability. There have been exceptions, and some very young mounts, like old Tom Jordan's Jake, were excellent performing horses.

18
Keep Your Cinches Tight!

Have you ever thought about the tremendous power a horse possesses? About the great strength he can muster up—for better or for worse—in a split second? All you riders with savvy have, and you are careful to do the right thing at the right time around a horse. You listen to the advice of expert horsemen and respect the horse for what he is—an animal that can respond to his rider's cues but cannot reason. So you keep your cinches tight when you ride.

Now when I say tight, I do not mean you must cut your horse in half. Just pull up, easy-like, until your saddle is down snug on your horse's back and you can still squeeze a couple of fingers between the mohair and the horse hair. Now mount up, ride around a minute, dismount, and give another short tug. This will settle your saddle nicely and take up that slack that comes from your horse's swelling when you first cinched him.

Of course, you see a lot of riders jogging along with loose cinches. Sometimes the cinch is just flopping, with enough space between it and the horse's underline for a pancake griddle. Usually these riders are sure of their horses and are good riders with excellent balance. Nevertheless, I think they are taking an unnecessary chance, just because a horse cannot reason. And no matter where you ride in these times, something strange can pop up to scare your horse.

I heard a story out of Arizona that is a good example of what can happen to any modern rider. A big air base in Tucson creates a lot of flying activity all year around. Well, a cowboy—and a good one—was just riding around his boss's ranch when a fast fighter jet came roaring overhead pretty close to the ground. The horse spooked. Then the shadow of the plane passed right over the spot where the horse was

A saddle that slips will leave its rider on the ground and be kicked to pieces by a lively horse.

Ike Rude, the famous Oklahoma steer roper, waits his turn at a Clovis, New Mexico, roping with his cinches snug. He will tighten them up beneath Buster, by Beggar Boy, before he ropes. The Cross J brand on the left hip means a good horse.

fidgeting. That did it. The horse, already nervous, shied violently to one side to escape that shadow. The loose-cinched saddle slid down the horse's flank and the cowboy found himself in the dirt watching his pony head for the ranch. That horse might have broken the quarter-mile track record if the dangling saddle had not slowed him down. The saddle finally dropped off, a battered wreck, and the cowboy had a long and tiresome walk carrying it back to the ranch.

So tight cinches are very important, not only for the rider's peace of mind, but also because they are absolutely necessary for horse sports—like polo, cutting, or roping. How far do you think big-time steer ropers would get if they left the chute box loose-cinched? Would it be possible for a top-rate duck-'n'-dive cattle cutter to block a steer successfully with his rider in a loose-cinched saddle? Are team ropers particular about their cinches? You bet they are.

I was roping at a friend's practice arena a few years back, team-tying steers. I thought my cinch was sufficiently tight. My friend was going to the steer's heels on a stout sorrel horse that really shifted into high gear when his rider connected and jabbed the spurs into him. I laid a loop around both horns of a wild, fast-running steer and turned off to the left. My pal scooted in on the sorrel and picked up both hind legs and took off in the opposite direction. *Wham!* With an awful creaking of leather and stretching of ropes, the horses were jerked to a stop by the steer-connected ropes. Just as I bailed out of the saddle to make the tie, the sorrel pulled my pony over backwards. He came up struggling, with the saddle pulled halfway down his back. Naturally, he panicked into a dead run, but with the weight of the steer and the sorrel acting as anchors, all my horse could manage was a big circle. Around and around he pounded, with the saddle slipping further and further down and the breast collar beginning to choke him. After a few hectic minutes I finally grabbed the bridle reins and stopped the whole mess. After that, I checked my cinches carefully.

If you are engaged in any strenuous activity with your horse, like roping or cutting, be sure you have strong cinches fore and aft. When a horse collects himself to turn a heifer, or braces himself against the jerks of a steer, or prepares for a quick stop, his belly muscles tighten and expand. This sudden expansion can snap a weak or worn cinch like a frayed string.

I was recently visiting a southern Arizona cattle ranch, watching the cowboys cull a few young bulls out of a herd. In that kind of work, a cutting horse simply whirls one way or the other in a kind of blocking or holding operation. Some of them are as quick as rattlers. One of the horses swiftly blocked a little bull. Then the saddle started to slip, and in a second that horse was high-rolling all over the corral. His rider got free in a hurry, but the horse continued his bucking spree until he had blasted the saddle right out from underneath him. After the dust had settled, the cowboys found that the part of the saddle rigging that holds the D ring in place had either slipped or torn when the horse jumped sideways.

You should be extra sure that your children's riding stock is cinched up well when the kids start crawling into the saddle. No matter how gentle and good-natured an old pony is, a slipping saddle is something that usually makes the most dog-headed of them get a kind of funny look in his eye.

The inexperienced rider, too, should always ride with a tight cinch, for the inexperienced rider is the rider without balance, and a rider without balance can easily upset a saddle. Once balance is learned, a looser cinch is okay. Lots of riders have jogged along with loose cinches for years and years, and will probably continue to do so. But for me, I like a little security down under the belly. I cannot help thinking about that jet fighter plane.

19
How to Select a Quarter Horse Stallion

Within each breed of horse there exists wide variances in type. The more popular the breed and the more different activities performed on the breed, then, I believe, the more varied in type the breed becomes. This is especially true today of America's two favorites, the Quarter Horse and the Thoroughbred (annually the Quarter Horse registry and the Jockey Club, Thoroughbred registry, register more horses than do other equine breed registries).

So, in selecting a stallion—either to buy or simply to use the services of—I would suggest that the prospective breeder be absolutely certain of what he wants his horses to do, and then select the type of stallion that he feels will produce these kinds of horses.

The late Colonel Fred L. Hamilton, a retired remount officer who used to live in Tucson, Arizona, was very keen on this point. He once received a letter from a friend, asking: "What stallion shall I breed my mares to?" The Colonel wrote back post haste: "Before I can answer that question I've got to know what you want your horses to do."

Colonel Hamilton said: "There are two common faults in horse breeding today. One is that people don't seem to know what they're breeding for. And the other is mismating in horse breeding. So many Thoroughbred breeders strive for speed and staying ability in their foals. To have both is extremely rare. In horse breeding you can't have your cake and eat it, too."

Ronald Mason, Thoroughbred and Quarter Horse breeder from Nowata, Oklahoma, also believes a man should have a purpose in mind before he starts to breed horses. He says:

"If I was going to buy a stallion there are many things I would take into consideration, for when you buy one you must buy him for a

No matter how excellent a stallion is, he should have good mares in his court. Here is a great mare from the past—Jole Blon, once owned by Glen Casey of Amarillo, Texas.

purpose. You would want him to sire good horses, either for showing, racing, roping, cutting—or just a good, sensible using horse. Now if I was in need of a stud that was bred right, looked right, and transmitted to his get his good qualities, I would buy him and wouldn't let a few dollars stand in my way.

"You must remember, however, that the mare side is very important, and no set of mares are uniform in conformation and bloodlines. So it's pretty hard to find one stallion that will cross with all mares and produce what you want in the get. In fact you have to experiment more or less to find out what nicks with what.

"I once had four stallions that I bred to Quarter mares—three registered Quarter sires and one Thoroughbred sire. If I have a mare to be bred, I try to figure out which stallion will nick best with this particular mare. As I have bred practically all my brood mares—also my stallions—I know their bloodlines, and it doesn't take long for me to decide what stallions to breed to.

"Another thing about buying a stallion: I wouldn't buy one just because he was pretty, fat, and slick. I would want one with speed in his veins, sense in his head, because sense in a horse is no good unless he has speed, and speed is no good without handling sense to go with it. They need both."

The two main points on which to select a stallion, after you have decided to what mares and for what purpose you are going to breed him, are conformation (this includes bodily soundness) and pedigree.

First off, a Quarter Horse stallion should be robust and masculine. He should look like a stud from his head to his hock. An effeminate stud should be avoided at all costs. The ideal stud, regardless of breed, should possess certain desirable traits—such as a well-balanced, athletic body; a well-proportioned, alert head, with large, kind, velvety eyes; a long, powerful neck that should join a wide, strong chest and smooth, sloping shoulders; well-defined withers, sloping into a strong,

Another great mare was Sage Hen, who dropped at least six or eight truly fine roping and reining mounts.

straight back, joining a long, neatly turned croup; straight legs, with solid bone and well-muscled forearms and gaskins; and sloping pasterns (not too short) above a good, solid, well-shaped hoof.

In moving out, the way of going of a prospective stud should be closely observed for unsoundness. It goes without saying that an unsound horse, where the unsoundness is of a congenital nature, is little more than worthless for breeding purposes.

The horse should move lightly and supply, with all his working parts performing their functions smoothly and properly. I am very high on a horse's athletic ability. A breeding horse should not only look like an athlete, but should act like one—at the walk, trot, lope, and gallop. It is easy to tell an active horse from an inactive, careless-moving, or lazy horse.

Think back to your high school or college days. Compare some of the characters you remember to some of the horses you are familiar

Speedywood, a stallion by Driftwood, is owned by Dale Smith of Chandler, Arizona. He is a good performer himself and thus would be a good horse to breed to a mare if you wanted a rope horse.

Fred Darnell, New Mexico roper and rancher, used to rope on Carrot, a Quarter Horse stallion who got some top roping colts. *Courtesy Matt Culley.*

with. What made some young men outstanding athletes, while others were hopelessly uncoordinated? Balance, symmetry, grace in motion, and a general awareness and alertness for things physical. The same characteristics can be applied to equine athletes as well as humans.

Pedigree and bloodlines, showing the ancestry of your prospective stallion and recording how his ancestors looked and performed, are of primary importance nowadays. This phase of stallion selection is also the most foolproof and easiest.

As a buyer, you may look at conformation and say to yourself, "That stud should do the job." But conformation alone will not always do the job. On the other hand, you can consult many generations of bloodlines, then check up on the individuals concerned to see what they were like. If they were all racehorses, for instance, with terrific early speed, then nine times out of ten the progeny of the stallion you are considering will have early speed, too—if the genes in the mare happen to nick right. There are a lot of "ifs" in the horse-breeding business.

Sid Vail, California horse breeder, once said of his great stallion, Three Bars: "I bought the horse for three reasons: bloodlines for speed, conformation to get good-looking foals, and the disposition to get quiet, well-mannered foals."

In the Quarter Horse industry today, you will find a great abundance of stallions to choose from. If choice is difficult because of the overwhelming number of available studs, your best course is to select an already-proven animal. It is a relatively simple matter, with a little work involved in checking the voluminous records kept of stallions, to find the ones that have consistently produced what you want.

A horseman really does not have to guess about breeding horses today. He could do it all by the record book and more often than not come out ahead. Of course, there will always be arguments and differences of opinion. That makes horse racing, so they say. It also adds interest and stimulation to all other horseback activities.

Experimentation, too, will still continue; it is healthy for the horse-breeding business. From experiments in the past have come many of the rules of thumb for modern breeders.

To sum up, the following suggestions may help those of you who may be in search of a stallion: (1) Clearly define your breeding program and its purpose before you make your stud selection; (2) Select a stud that is a typey, masculine representative of the breed, be sure he is sound, be sure he is (or was) an athlete; (3) Try to visualize the kind of colts the stallion will get when crossed with your mares; (4) Check the record book to see if he has produced what you are looking for; and (5) Check his bloodlines and his pedigree and his family line, individual by individual on both male and female sides, as far back as you can.

20
Buying and Selling Quarter Horses

In the June, 1972, issue of the *Quarter Horse Journal* there was a listing of sixty-two forthcoming public Quarter Horse auctions in nineteen states and Canada. A lot of horses up for sale? You bet. Estimating that each auction offered eighty-five head for sale (a very conservative figure), simple multiplication reveals that 5,270 individual horses, mares, colts, and fillies were offered to interested buyers.

One of the biggest sales included in the listing—and also represented with a thirty-page ad in the *Journal* (a replica of the complete catalog)—was the M. J. Coen Farms Complete Dispersal at Kansas City, Missouri.

Quarter Horse sales, as you can see, are big business and are either listed or advertised (or both) in most horse magazines. And I emphasize this somewhat to point out that the easiest and quickest way to get into the Quarter Horse game is to attend a Quarter Horse sale and buy. At the Coen Farms sale you could have purchased 137 head if you had so desired and were financed with unlimited resources. You could have bid on a horse or two without even being there. And this is the way that little gambit works:

At the back of the Coen Farms *Journal* advertisement, a printed coupon gave the following information to stay-at-home bidders: "If you cannot attend this sale personally, we urge you to complete this bid form on any lot or lots you are interested in and forward it to us. Your confidence will be respected." Then there appeared four spaces to enter the numbers of four lots of horses and jot down the fees that you would have considered reasonable and that you would have been willing to pay had your bids held up at the time of auction. The coupon

There is nothing like proving the tractability of a horse to a prospective buyer. If you know the buyer wants a children's horse, pull a kid into the saddle with you.

wound up with these instructions: "A check for 25% of the mail bid must accompany this letter. If the bid (or bids) is successful, the remainder of the purchase price must be forwarded upon notice from the seller." Naturally, if your estimate of the worth of the horse in question had been low, and you were outbidden, your check would have been returned.

Because the terms and conditions—again referring to the Coen Farms sale ad—are so similar to most Quarter sales, let's look at that advertisement again:

1. Terms of sale are for cash. Payment for horses purchased is to be made immediately after the sale. Please be sure that the clerk has the correct name and address as all registration certificates will be mailed by the buyers.
2. The highest bidder is the buyer. If any dispute arises between two or more bidders, the horse in dispute shall immediately be put up again for advance bid between the disputing bidders. If there is no advance, then the horse shall go to the person whose bid the auctioneer has recognized.
3. Each animal will be inspected as it enters the sale ring. All known blemishes or defects will be announced before the bidding starts. Each broodmare in the sale will have been pregnancy examined prior to the sale. Those who are not in foal will be announced from the auction stand and sold without further guarantee unless so stated while in the auction ring. Those sold in foal carry no further guarantee except that the buyer may have the mare examined by a veterinarian within 24 hours of the sale and prior to the removal from M. J. Coen Farms. If such a mare is found to be open, she will be declared unsold. There will be no returns to any stallion as they are included in the offering and will be sold.
4. M. J. Coen Farms will care for the animal 24 hours after the sale, at the purchaser's risk. If a purchaser cannot take delivery within 24 hours, M. J. Coen Farms will care for the animal for a reasonable period if satisfactory arrangements are made in advance.
5. Every effort has been made to assure correctness of the catalogue but the owners, sales personnel and auctioneer will not be responsible for errors or omissions and assume no liability on their part as to any statements, either verbal or written, regarding horses sold. All statements and catalogue corrections announced at the sale shall supersede the catalogue.

In alphabetical order I present some of the prominent individuals and firms that specialize in Quarter Horse sales. If you want to buy, or if you want to consign a horse to a sale, contact the man or company closest to your home.

At riding clubs or public training stables there are always a few good horses for sale or trade.

Ada QH Sales, Inc. (Pete Winters or Doyle Mathews), Box 1385, Ada, Oklahoma.

Max Bixler, Box 162, Waynoka, Oklahoma.

Blue Ribbon QH Sale Co. (Harold McIlrath, Jim Jeffords and Joe Lindholm), P. O. Box 162, Audubon, Iowa.

California Mid-Winter QH Sales, Inc. (Tom Caldwell or Dale Rouk), 1357 Euclid Street, Ontario, California 91763.

John Carlile Co., P. O. Box 2111, Amarillo, Texas 79105.

C. A. Cofer, 3641 N. Maize Road, Wichita, Kansas 67205.

Jerry Graham, Route 1, Rocheport, Missouri.

Ike Hamilton, 2025 Hicks Street, West Monroe, Louisiana.

Gordon Hannagan, Plainfield, Illinois.

Haymaker Sales Co. (Dale and Chet Robertson) R. R. 2, Box 221, Yukon, Oklahoma 73009.

Bill Hedge, Sallisaw, Oklahoma.

Dean H. Parker & Associates, Route 2, Box 2273, Auburn, California 95603.

Bob Plummer Sales Management, Box 926, Henderson, Texas 75652.

Buddy Reger, Box 954, Woodward, Oklahoma.

Bob Roper, c/o Vernon Roper, Onia, Arkansas 72663.

Arizona racehorse trainer Manny Figueroa pauses briefly while exercising a pair of short-distance speedsters that have a combination of Quarter Horse and Thoroughbred blood in their veins.

Bill Smale Sale Management, 120 Lyford Drive, Tiburon, California 94920. Whitman Sales Co. (Carol A. Whitman), P. O. Box 143, Carthage, Missouri.

If you like to travel, another way of seeking out horses to purchase is to visit as many breeding farms and ranches as you can on a two- or three-week trip, or even on your vacation. But plan ahead; find out something about the establishment at which you will be stopping. You would not want to look over a ranch that raises racing stock if you have decided that what you want to buy are halter show animals.

Be sure to preserve mentally your experiences while in the process of buying horses. Take note of those things that impressed you, while remembering those things that were distasteful to you. For someday you, too, if you get deeply involved in the business of enjoying Quarter Horses, will be selling horses yourself.

So recall your own reactions to situations and realize that people buy what they see only if they like what they see. This is true of anything—houses, land, automobiles, boats, or horses. When you go to sell a horse, play up the good features and play down those features, if there are any, that may not be so good.

Do not misunderstand me. You should not try to bamboozle a buyer. If there is anything wrong—like thrush, a disease of the frog of the hoof, be sure to point this out. It is much better for you to tell the truth to your buyer than for him to discover the ailment later on. After all, you may want to sell him, or his friends, another horse or two some day. To keep selling, your reputation as a dealer must be unblemished.

Animals for sale should be well groomed and healthy looking. Hooves should be trimmed and, if the horse is going to be shown under saddle, they should be well shod by an experienced farrier. Your horse's mane should either be clipped or neatly combed. The tail should be combed out, with any excess growth clipped from around the tail root. Your horse should look as sleek and attractive as possible to the prospective buyer.

Choose an experienced rider—either yourself, your son, or a capable hand—to show the horse under saddle. If you do not make a good appearance on a horse, admit it and put somebody in the saddle who does.

By all means let your buyer try the horse out for himself if he wants to. Or let him put some one of his own choice in the saddle. Whatever the buyer wants to do with the horse, within reason, should be acceptable to you. And always remember that a satisfied buyer is apt to return. He will certainly tell others about your horse and where he bought him.

21
Thoroughbred Blood in the Quarter Horse

Thoroughbred blood is again upgrading the Quarter Horse, for short-speed racing anyway, just as "Oriental" blood did in Colonial times (see Chapter 9). For several decades now, short horse enthusiasts have been using the services of Thoroughbred stallions with short-speed pedigrees.

One of the truly great ones that made a lasting impression on the Quarter Horse was the late Three Bars, owned by Californian Sid Vail. It is interesting to note that of the first four leading sires of AQHA Register of Merit qualifiers (1945–71), three are Thoroughbreds and one is a Quarter Horse sired by a Thoroughbred. And Three Bars, a Thoroughbred, heads up the list with 528 foals, 424 starters, and 315 Register of Merit qualifiers. (Next is Go Man Go by Top Deck, a Thoroughbred; third is Rocket Bar, a Thoroughbred; fourth is Top Deck, a Thoroughbred.)

Three Bars was foaled on the Monterey Farm at Paris, Kentucky. His mother, Myrtle Dee, had been purchased at the Jim Parrish Dispersal by Monterey Farm owners Ned Brant and Bill Talbot and trainer Jack Goode. The mare was safe in foal to Percentage by Midway by Ballot by Voter, and when, on April 8, 1940, the little red colt dropped they all put their heads together and named him Three Bars—because they were all sure they had hit the jackpot.

Percentage, Three Bars' sire, who was out of Gossip Avenue by Bulse by Disguise, was a fast horse and won nineteen races in his early years. Myrtle Dee, the dam, was also a winner at two, three, and five years of age. She was by Luke McLuke out of Civil Maid by Patriotic by American Flag by Man O' War. Luke McLuke's sire was Ultimus by Commando by Domino.

Sid Vail is shown holding the late Three Bars, a Thoroughbred that singularly influenced the breeding of straightaway speedsters.

Three Bars' own race career was undistinguished. The horse was very fast, with amazing early speed, but after his workouts his hind leg would stiffen up and become as cold as ice. The next day he would be normal again. As a three-year-old he won one race in one start. As a four-year-old he won three races in four starts. In the early part of his fourth year at Hot Springs, Arkansas, he fell coming out of the gate, bursting one knee open and losing a few teeth. But making a remarkable recovery, he got back up onto his feet and was able to beat three of the horses to the finish line in a twelve-horse field.

As a youngster, he had stifled himself (the movable bone forming the anterior part of the stifle joint was displaced), which did not add to his brilliance on the track. In fact, Three Bars in his early days was a very frustrating animal to the men who tried to race him: he could run—run like the wind with a bolt of lightning chasing it—but he would not stay sound. When Jack Goode first took the horse to Chicago, Goode's father, also a very noted trainer in Thoroughbred racing circles, said he thought he was the fastest horse he had ever seen.

When the trouble became so bad that Three Bars would not even stay sound after workouts, Goode sold him to a man named Beck Stiver for three hundred dollars out of his first win (under Stiver's ownership). Stiver, in turn, became so frustrated and disgusted that he finally gave Three Bars away to a blacksmith. In his fourth year, at Detroit, he was claimed by R. S. Snedigar and D. M. Haggard, who brought the horse to Phoenix, Arizona, to rest him and see if it would be possible for him to race again.

Three Bars seemed to like the Arizona climate, and in 1946, at the Phoenix Fairgrounds, he worked out over a mile and a quarter distance as fast as the track record at Hollywood Park. Then Sid Vail bought the horse. Sid was then living in Douglas, Arizona, and he leased him back to Snedigar and Haggard. In 1947, Three Bars was one of only three American horses invited by the Brazilian Jockey Club to run in the fifty-thousand-dollar Grand Prix at a mile and seven-eighths. But Three Bars was then retired from racing and beginning to gain a little publicity as a sire.

Along about this time several Arizona breeders, including Melville Haskell, J. Rukin Jelks, Bob Locke, and others, were not only interested in producing good horseflesh but were also vitally stimulated by the challenge from the short-distance track. The sport of Quarter Horse racing had just started in the Southwest, and sportsmen and ranchers were trying to find the answer to the challenge, the answer to short speed.

They thought the solution was in high-quality, speed-bred Thoroughbreds (many of them still do), and horses like Piggin String, Marco Way, Top Deck, Depth Charge, Spotted Bull, and Three Bars became famous overnight, so to speak, once a colt or two ran and triumphed at one of the traditional Quarter Horse distances.

Of all the Thoroughbred Quarter Horses—and just a very few have been named—Three Bars has been the most successful in all categories. And one category that is not talked about too much, for the horse is primarily a sire of running horses, is the conformation category. Three Bars' offspring are more often than not good-looking Quarter Horses. They are darned good-looking Quarter Horses. Whether they have perfect Quarter Horse conformation is a question open for debate. But they look to most knowledgeable horsemen like horses that can do something. They look like equine athletes—and they were and are that very thing.

Take Art Pollard's wonderful stud Lightning Bar as a case in point. Here was a son of Three Bars (out of Della P) who, until his untimely death, was destined to become perhaps as great a sire as his father. Lightning Bar was a big, beautiful, powerful horse. He was an amazing and terrific looking individual, and although he showed some Quarter Horse characteristics, his complete physical makeup was not what some Quarter Horse people would call ideal.

But Three Bars came closer than any Thoroughbred horse that I know of to producing acceptable Quarter Horse conformation and Quarter Horse speed. Many times in the past his get have stood high in colt and filly classes. At Los Alamitos once, the first six horses in a 400-yard race were sons of Three Bars. One time at Rillito Park in Tucson, five of his get coheld the 330-yard mark of :17.3. In 1957, Three Bars was a subject of Ripley's *Believe It Or Not,* when his sons, Big Bar, Lux Bar, and Gray Bar, finished one, two, and three in the sixth race in November, 1956, at Los Alamitos.

Melville Haskell, an Arizonan who was responsible for formulating the regulations of Quarter Horse racing, has never concealed in any way his enthusiasm for the Thoroughbred. When I asked him several years ago what influence he felt Thoroughbred blood had on the modern-day Quarter Running Horse, he said: "As far as I'm concerned it's made the Quarter Running Horse. If you don't believe it, all you have to do is go through the pedigree papers of the top horses for the past ten years to see how much Thoroughbred blood they have in them."

The 1971 leading money-earning owner of racing Quarter Horses was Will F. Whitehead of Del Rio, Texas, with $301,280. His Mr. Kid Charge, a sorrel colt foaled in 1969—and a grandson of Three Bars—accounted for most of these earnings ($268,398.40) and was the winner of the Ruidoso Downs All-American Futurity. Mr. Kid Charge was also the 1971 AQHA Champion Quarter Running Two-Year-Old Colt.

The 1971 leading breeder of winners was A. B. Green of Purcell, Oklahoma, with winners accounting for $288,824.

The breeder who had the most winners in 1971 was Guy Ray Rutland of Independence, Kansas, with 128 wins at 440 yards or under.

The leading breeder of AQHA Register of Merit qualifiers on the racetrack was Bud Warren of Perry, Oklahoma, with 151.

And for further evidence of Thoroughbred blood in Quarter Horses causing extreme early speed, let's end this chapter by looking at the partial pedigrees of some of the 1971 running champs. For instance

Many foals, like this good-looking youngster, are of substantial Thorough-bred blood yet can be registered and raced as Quarter Horses.

Bunny Bid, the champion Quarter Racing Stallion, is by Double Bid by Double Feature, Thoroughbred.

The undefeated racing champ for 1971 (listed in Chapter 28), Charger Bar, goes back on her sire's side to the Thoroughbred Depth Charge. Kaweah Bar, the champion Quarter Horse Gelding, goes back on his sire's side to Three Bars. Kaweah Bar, owned by George Chittick of Long Beach, California, won $241,521 in 1971.

Osage Rocket, champion Quarter Running Filly, goes back to Three Bars through her sire Rocket Bar, himself a Thoroughbred. Come Six, champion Quarter Running Gelding (two-year-old), also is by a Thoroughbred, Azure, who is by Nashville.

And Jet Injun, champion Quarter Racing Stallion, goes back on his sire's side to the Thoroughbred Top Deck. Top Deck sired Moon Deck who sired Jet Deck (deceased), who is Jet Injun's father.

22
Logging Pays Off

Two of the most challenging roping contests in modern rodeo are single steer roping and steer team tying. Historically, they are the oldest forms of horse-and-cowboy roping, originating out of necessity many years ago on the open ranges of the Southwest cattle country. Due to the tendency to streamline rodeo today, these two events are not often programmed except in those parts of the country where people understand them and like to watch them.

A number of reasons automatically eliminate steer roping and team tying from most rodeos and horse shows, including the sizable expense of leasing the right kind of cattle, the small size of many arenas, and pressure from certain factions that would like to see all hard-and-fast steer roping banned. But to a small and dedicated group of rodeo cowboys, men who by the very nature of their work have been and are real cowboys, roping steers singlehandedly or with a partner is the greatest sport in the world. (Head-and-heels team roping has the blessings of the AQHA for horse show inclusion.)

It is also a fiercely competitive sport, so the professionals and semi-professionals of tie-down roping must use the best horses they can get their hands on—horses that are not only powerful and dependable, but ones that have been or can be trained with logs.

We would say that nowadays all single steer horses and most team-tying head horses, at one time or another in their careers, have been schooled in the exacting art of dragging heavy logs.

"Logging," says Arizonan Roy Wales, "is good for any young horse that you're going to rope on. It teaches him how to handle weight. And you can show him a lot more with the dead weight of a log than you can with the live weight of an animal."

The late Bud Parker comes in to rope the heels of this fast-running steer. If the header's horse has been properly logged, the sudden jerk that seems imminent will not bother him. *Courtesy Chuck Abbott.*

Wales, like most horsemen, breaks his prospective rope horse stock as two-year-olds, and in several months, when they are good and gentle, he starts logging them. At first he uses very light logs, weighing no more than 150 pounds. The young horses drag these logs at a walk, getting the feel of the weight pulling on the saddle horn and instinctively learning how to walk against the drag, using their own body weight to their best advantage.

One of the main purposes of logging young horses is to rid them of any fear they might have of being attached to something heavy. A young horse that has not been logged might justifiably throw a fit upon finding himself attached for the first time to a jumping calf or steer. A logged horse would at least be accustomed to the weight, if not the movement.

Since calf horses back up on the rope, steadied and kept straight by the use of a neck rope, light logs such as railroad cross ties are employed as training aids. But any movable object can be used.

One year the veteran roper, Ike Rude, took Baldy, his great gelding, back to New York's Madison Square Garden rodeo. Quite a few boys were mounted on Baldy and, of course, Ike wanted the horse to win as much as he could. So every day between performances Ike schooled Baldy on the heavy, three-cornered harrow that was used to disk up the arena turf. He would fasten his rope to it and then holler, "Back up, Baldy! Back up!" And Baldy backed. He backed so well that he helped every roper who was riding him take away part of the calf-roping money.

Since steers are bigger than calves and there is no guiding device, like a neck rope, when the header laces his rope around a steer's horns and reins away, logging pays off even more when it comes to training for heavy roping. Here is a way a lot of cowboys introduce their prospective steer horses to the log: To the rings of a snaffle bit they attach two long light lines. They operate these just as if they were driving a buggy horse. From the bit rings, the lines come straight back beside the fork of the saddle through other rings or through pulleys. Standing on the ground behind the horse that is pulling the log, the trainer has complete control of his colt. He can keep him from moving too fast by pulling on both lines; he can keep him on a straight course by plow reining one line or the other; or he can keep him moving by flicking him on the rump with both lines.

This method has proved to be successful all over the country where horses are trained for single roping or for heading in team tying. However, trainers like Wales say that the utmost patience must be taken with a young horse so that he is not frightened or overlogged. "A long training period of repetition," he says, "is far better for a young horse than trying to pound it into his head in a short time."

As the colt matures and becomes acquainted with his work, and as he graduates from the snaffle to a regular bit, preferably one with a bar across the bottom of the shanks, the guide lines are removed. In their place, and rigged onto the left side of the saddle in the same way, through a ring or a pulley, comes one line, called a stop- or jerk-line, tied to the center of the bit bar.

By this time the horse may or may not have roped steers, but he should be working well on the log. The trainer should have confidence in his ability. The trainer lopes him out against the weight of the log and dismounts. The horse, feeling the weight, digs into it. If the horse should overwork or overpull the log, the trainer can jerk the stopline and yell, "Whoa!" He can also throw himself down on the log, adding to its weight.

Single steer horses are trained to pull as hard as they can for a short

Ben Johnson (an Oscar winner for the hero figure in *The Last Picture Show*) adjusts his rope while logging one of his steer horses some years ago.

distance after the roper has left the saddle. They must keep the steer sledding along until the roper can reach it. Since it is far better for a horse to overwork than to quit pulling at the crucial moment when the steer is struggling to get up, a few ropers use stoplines on horses in actual roping competition. As it dangles behind the horse, the roper can grab it on his way to the steer or after he gets there, stopping the horse's forward motion if he continues to overwork.

Heavy logs are used in advanced training for steer horses. In single steer roping, two sudden jerks hit the saddle horn as the rope becomes taut. The first is the trip, when the steer is lifted off the ground, and the second, known as the bust, occurs when the steer hits the ground. In heading steers for a partner to heel, there are also usually two such split-second moments of quick heavy tugs.

To simulate these two sudden pulls, horses with their full growth and strength are run against two logs tied together by a short rope or chain. The time element between the actual trip and bust of a steer and the quick pulls received from the two logs is about the same. The pull from the light log—about 150 pounds—comes first; the second pull, an instant pull, is harder, usually from a log of 300 pounds.

Logs vary in weight according to the size of the horses being trained and the size of the stock for which a roper is schooling his horse. Most trainers agree that five hundred pounds is about the limit. A few use heavier logs, a few use lighter ones. Some trainers prefer round logs, like telephone poles, pilings, or tree trunks, which roll or sled over the ground more smoothly than sharp-cornered logs. Some like square-cut logs because they can stand on them more easily.

But no matter what kinds of logs, or any other types of weights used, the idea is basically the same: to teach horses what weight is, how to handle it, and to take heavy jerks. Ropers want horses that will go to the end of the rope with power and stay there, bracing against any pull.

Some horses learn quickly after a few months of logging and never have to be logged again. Other horses, with poorer memories, are logged all the time or just before going to a rodeo. Still others, spoiled

Ben Johnson watches the heavy log as his horse pulls away for all the sorrel gelding's worth. This work trains horses for handling heavy steers.

or stubborn horses, have to be logged to offset bad habits. Logging works both ways. It is mostly used as a training aid to make a horse work, but sometimes it has to be used to cure a horse that overworks.

Wales once owned a bay gelding that was so badly spoiled that every time he went to the end of a rope he kept running at full speed, trying to break loose. He was completely unmanageable, useless for roping, and nothing would stop him. He ran away with cattle, ran off with logs, tore saddles apart, and broke ropes.

Finally in desperation, for the horse was a good one and had once been a top roping mount, Wales decided on a last resort. He took the bay down into a dry, sandy wash and tied one end of a sixty-foot nylon rope to a husky limb of a tamarisk tree, growing on the bank of the wash. He tied the other end hard and fast to the saddle horn. The horse's breast collar was perfectly adjusted so as not to choke him and the saddle was cinched up tight.

Holding the coils of nylon in his right hand, Wales headed the horse down the wash, away from the tree, and stepped off, feeding the coils to the bay as the spoiled gelding broke away at a dead run.

"I threw the last couple of coils after him," said Wales, "and got out of there as fast as I could. It was the darndest thing you ever saw. That old tree limb bent about as far as it would go and the nylon stretched about as far as it would go. Then that limb whipped back into place and the stretch sucked back out of the rope and the horse was lifted right off his feet straight over backwards into the sand.

"It didn't hurt him any because it was a nice soft fall, but it sure surprised him. Believe me, after a few more applications of that medicine, that old pony respected a rope and quit trying to run off every time he went to the end of one."

Occasionally you hear of somebody working his horse tied to a heavy snubbing post set in the ground. A poor method, say the logging men, for you are apt to break ropes, tear up saddles, and, worse, cripple your horse as he runs against a weight that has no give to it. The big advantage of a log is that a horse can move it, just as he should do with live cattle at the end of his training period.

The perfectly trained horse will move against the rope, his rump toward the weight, bracing himself and surging forward as he receives the full impact. In single roping, he will drag the steer until the roper gets it under control for the tie. Then the horse will hold it down. In team tying, his rider will not dismount until the heeler has made his catch. When the rider does jump off, the horse should hustle to the end of the rope and then, feeling the weight hit him, should brace and hold steady. No horse in any roping event should ever give slack, for a slack rope enables a steer to move its head and neck, letting it kick.

Good, sensible logging teaches a horse the basics before he ever chases a steer. He knows about weight on the rope and angles and sudden jerks. Half his training is over. Thanks to the heavy log training, steer roping and team-tying runs are getting faster and faster.

23
Some Other Things to Do on Quarter Horses

I do not like to repeat myself over a dozen times in describing the versatility of the Quarter Horse. So for the thirteenth and last time: the main thing that makes the Quarter Horse so great is the fact that anybody can do just about anything on his sturdy back. In the preceding chapters I have already talked about his skill as a cow horse, a rope horse, a polo horse, a cutting horse, a racehorse, a simple pleasure horse, and a show horse.

There are still a lot of other things people do on Quarter Horses—organized sports and competitions—and I want to look at some of these:

BARREL RACING: This sport has become so refined that it has its own organization and circuit of approved contests. The group is called the Girls Rodeo Association, after their brethren in the Rodeo Cowboys Association. Although there are a few all-girl rodeos—consisting of most of the main events in regular men's rodeos—for the most part the girls are satisfied with several hundred barrel racings a year at horse shows and rodeos. Some of these offer fat purses. The 1972 Cheyenne Frontier Days put up a thousand-dollar purse, to which all fifty-dollar entry fees were added. The current GRA secretary is Edith Connelly, 187 Mountain Home Road, Woodside, California 94062.

Some of the more experienced cowgirls, like Nevada's Sammy Fancher Thurman, hold barrel racing clinics in the spring and summer at various towns on the barrel racing rodeo circuit. In 1972 Sammy's clinics were held in May and June at Chinle, Arizona; Lewiston, Montana; Rawlins, Wyoming; Berthoud, Colorado; and Polson, Montana.

Norita Henderson, a past GRA barrel-racing champion from Valley Park, Missouri, pours it on as she rounds a barrel on a top Quarter Horse. *Courtesy Bern Gregory.*

As in all equine sports, the horse is the basic ingredient for the excitement. Competition goes like this: Each girl and her Quarter Horse race around a three-barrel course, commencing with a barrel (1) at the right of the start/finish line (an inside turn); then going straight across the course to a barrel (2) on the left of the start/finish line (another inside turn); and then going to the last barrel (3) centered about forty yards away from the other two. After making the turn on the third barrel from right to left, the rider races straight back to the finish line. Each rider races against the hands of a stopwatch and the fastest time takes the top money. Contestants are allowed a running start and, of course, they are also in high gear at the finish, crossing the line at full gallop. Barrels one and two are thirty-five yards apart and about twenty-five yards from the start/finish line.

Good barrel horses are well trained and command a lot of money. When a cowgirl buys or develops a top horse, she is not apt to part with it for any offer.

Sapphire Cody, owned by C. T. Fuller's Willow Brook Farms at Catasauqua, Pennsylvania, shows the reining form that won her the AQHA 1971 championship title in this event. Trainer Bob Anthony is up.

REINING: The official AQHA handbook describes four sanctioned reining patterns from which horse show managements may select, depending upon the size of arenas and the caliber of the performers. All the patterns consist of a combination of stops, turns, figure eights, spins, and circles to both right and left. The judge looks for poised and controlled horses that execute these maneuvers exceptionally well.

There are several state groups championing the reining horse, but the chief organization is the National Reining Horse Association with headquarters at 1290 Hine Road, Hamilton, Ohio 45013. The NRHA sponsors several contests each year, including the popular futurity. Since the demand for two-year-olds with reining potential is increasing, the

NRHA Futurity draws many equine youngsters. The 1970 futurity prize totalled twenty-two thousand dollars; the first place horse won three thousand dollars.

The NRHA's Sire and Dam Recognition Program is another phase in the promotion of the western-type working horse. Starting with the 1968 futurity, a trophy, cash, and publicity has been given annually to owners of the participating sires of colts and fillies placing first, second, and third in the futurity. In 1970, Poco Red Ant, the sire of the futurity winner, received some worthwhile publicity and his owner got a twelve-hundred-dollar check, plus an elegant trophy.

POLE BENDING: The pole bending pattern is usually run around a half dozen poles twenty-one feet apart. The first pole is set twenty-one feet from the starting line. All the poles must be set on top of the ground, not buried, on bases not over fourteen inches in diameter.

This is a timed event using western equipment. Horse and rider leave the start/finish line, race past all the poles and start around the poles at the top of the course. At the bottom of the course, they recircle all the poles toward the top and then race back to the start/finish line.

COLAS (tailing of the bull): This is a new AQHA-approved contest added to the handbook in 1972. We probably will not see much of it in the United States, but it has long been—and will continue to be—part of the colorful horsemanship of the Mexican *charros.*

Riders are judged on their skill in tailing the bull at full gallop, and also on horsemanship, color, costumes and showmanship. It is impossible to describe an event I have never seen, so I will just go along with the rules handbook, which states whenever any part of the animal touches the turf of the arena, it shall be considered a fall. Points are scored from twelve to six, depending upon how gracefully and in what position the bull is grounded.

CALA (reining of the horse) : This is another new AQHA contest aimed at our neighbors' shows south of the border. The test is a demonstration of the good training of the *charro* horse. Judges look for equine spirit, head and tail posture, tameness, gait, stirrup, good handling, and individual costuming.

CUTTER AND CHARIOT RACING: These events, performed mostly in the northwest part of the United States, are becoming increasingly popular and benefit from dual approval: they are AQHA-approved and also have their own association, which also approves the contests, called Cutter and Chariot Racing Association at Pocatello, Idaho. Devotees of the sport can subscribe to their own publication, *Cutter and Chariot Racing,* P. O. Box 896, Idaho Falls, Idaho 83401.

The contests consist of a series of races, matching two or more two-horse teams pulling a cutter and driver or chariot and driver. Cutter racing is done on ice; chariot racing on a dirt track.

Training, as in all forms of speed competition, is all important, and ranchers take great pride in producing top-speed pairs. (Horses that race on ice are shod with special shoes with calks to prevent slipping.)

WESTERN RIDING: This contest is neither a stunt nor a race. It is held to show off the performance of a "sensible, well-mannered, free-and-easy moving ranch horse, which can get the rider around on the usual ranch chores, over the trails, or give a quiet, comfortable and pleasant ride in open country through and over obstacles," according to the AQHA.

TRAIL HORSE: Let's let the AQHA handbook describe this approved event:

> The class will be judged on the performance of the horse at the three gaits [walk, trot and lope], performance over the obstacles, response to the rider, and intelligence. It is to be judged 60 per cent on work over the obstacles, 30 per cent on rail work, and 10 per cent on conformation.
>
> Mandatory obstacles are: 1. Opening, passing through, and closing gate. (Use a gate which will not endanger horse or rider.) 2. Ride over at least four logs. 3. Ride over wooden bridge.
>
> Optional obstacles are: 1. Water hazard (ditch or shallow pond). 2. Hobble or ground-tie horse. 3. Carry object from part of arena to another. (Only objects which reasonably might be carried on a trail ride may be used.) 4. Back horse through "L" shaped course. 5. Put on and remove slicker. 6. Dismount and lead horse over obstacles not less than 14 inches high or over 24 inches high. 7. Send horse freely into horse trailer. (This obstacle not allowed in Youth Activity.) [See chapter 27 for details of Youth Activity.]

WORKING COW HORSE: Again to quote from the AQHA:

> Both the cattle working part of this event and the reining part are mandatory. Scoring will be on the basis of 60 to 80, with 70 denoting an average performance. The same basis of scoring shall apply to both the reined work and cow work. Fall of horse and/or rider while being shown either in cow work or reined work shall not eliminate the entry.
>
> The following characteristics are considered as faults: A. Switching tail. B. Exaggerated opening of mouth. C. Hard or heavy mouth. D. Nervous throwing of head. E. Lugging on bridle. F. Halting or hesitation while being shown, particularly when being run out, indicating anticipation of being set up, which is characteristic of an overtrained horse. G. Losing a cow or being unable to finish a pattern because of a bad cow, the contestant should be penalized at the judge's discretion. H. Touching the horse or saddle with the free hand.
>
> The characteristics of a good working horse are: A. Good manners.

You can also rope steers on a Quarter Horse. Carl Arnold is shown dismounting from Breezy in a Laramie, Wyoming, contest. *Courtesy Orren Mixer.*

B. Horse should be shifty, smooth and have his feet under him at all times; when stopping, hind feet should be well under him. C. Horse should have a soft mouth and should respond to a light rein, especially when turning. D. Head should be maintained in its natural position. E. Horse should be able to work at reasonable speed and still be under control of the rider.

BRIDLE PATH HACK (saddle seat): A horse is to be shown at a walk, trot, and canter in horse show competition. The event is AQHA-approved.

BRIDLE PATH HACK (hunt seat): A horse is to be shown at a walk, trot, and canter in horse show competition. This event is AQHA-approved.

WORKING HUNTER: Horses will be worked through one of several approved courses. Judges will be responsible for the layout and correctness of each course.

JUMPING: Writing in the March, 1972, issue of the *Quarter Horse Journal,* Bobbie Meyers reemphasizes the do-it-all nature of the breed:

Zipper Cody, another Willow Brook Farms horse, won the AQHA 1971 junior English pleasure horse championship. Donna Anthony is the rider.

Long hailed as the most versatile of all using horses, one that could do it all, the Quarter Horse is again excelling in what is for him a relatively new field of endeavor. Open jumping competition by Quarter Horses has only been attempted in recent years. Yet, against heavy odds, two Quarter Horses won the Puissance Class and one went on to be named Jumper Champion at the National Western Stock Show & Rodeo at Denver in January.

According to the Funk-Wagnalls *New Practical Dictionary,* puissance is a word of French origin, meaning power and strength to achieve or accomplish. How better to describe a Quarter Horse? This typical power and strength carried Bassanio, a 14-year-old grey gelding owned and ridden by Charlie Phyllis Hughes of Denver, over a 6'3" brick wall and a 6'6" spread X 5'6" high triple bar to win his section of the Puissance Class. Excitement ran high the next night when Dr. No, whose registered name is Fubar, cleared the brick wall at 6'9" and a 7' spread on the triple bar to set a new record for the National Western and thus win the second section. Dr. No is owned by Carl Baker of Aurora, Colorado, and was ridden by Donna McGee.

Bassanio was also designated as Jumper Champion of the 1972 National Western after successfully competing in all five of the stake classes.

24
Advanced Training for Rope Horses

Horses can learn, but they cannot figure things out. They can be taught what to do and what not to do. But in the face of an unexpected crisis— like a fire in a stable—they are reduced to helpless panic. They learn only through repetition and association.

The mechanics of following a running calf is one of the easiest things to teach a horse, provided he is strong and healthy and well broken, say about three or four years old.

A horse has a natural desire to run and, I think, a horse has a natural, perhaps playful, desire to chase moving objects. Watch a bunch of frisky Quarter Horse colts playing in a pasture. Spook them and see what happens. They will take off with a rush, jumping and bucking, as they slow down from their first startled getaway. They are enjoying the run and they are also naturally following each other.

The same holds true for beginning rope horses. A horse will enjoy the run and the chase and in no time at all he will be following a calf and letting you take a throw at it. I do not think that an older rope horse really loves the work so much. By that time, if a horse is any-where from eight to twelve, the action of calf roping is just a chore, a job he has done so much that it is all automatic.

But in the first stages of training, a horse should be handled easily and gently and, if possible, be made to think it is fun. So do not overdo it and sour a good prospect.

Start out with slow calves and lope your horse after them for the first few days. Then, say on the fourth day, breeze him out of the box good and fast, reining him if need be, right up behind the calf. If this excites him too much, go back to slow calves. You do not want to make a horse race out of the training at the very start.

Fundamentally, a calf horse is made by cues and repetition. His ability and usefulness depend upon how fast he learns these cues and how well his trainer applies them. Naturally, horses and trainers vary considerably. I believe that it is much better to take a horse too slowly than too fast. The tendency is to hurry on with the training if the horse shows promise, and in some cases this is all right. But a word of caution: there have been more horses spoiled by too much hurry than have been turned into finished mounts.

Before you start roping and bailing off, your horse should be taught that he is supposed to stop. You can put the idea of stopping into his head in a few hours by cues and repetition. At a walk, suddenly shift your weight into the left stirrup, pull on the reins sharply just once, and then drop your left hand, your rein hand, onto the top of your horse's neck. By the way, the mane should be roached for two reasons: so you will not get your rope coils caught in it, and so that your horse will feel the pressure of your hand on the crest of his neck. As you do this, your hand dips to the saddle horn, grasps it, and you step off. Do this one hundred times at a walk and your horse will be stopping dead in his tracks without a jerk on the reins.

Next, go to a trot or a lope. Some trainers prefer to go directly from the walk into the lope, for they figure that a trot is a gait that rope horses seldom use, so there is no association. A gallop at full speed is no more than an accelerated lope or canter.

But no matter where you go from the lope, do the same thing: shift your weight, jerk the reins if you need to, knock your horse on the neck, and drop out of the saddle. Soon you will find that you will not have to touch the reins at all, that the cues of weight shifting and neck slapping are enough for the stop.

Now your horse knows how to follow and how to stop. But he will not, unless he is exceptional, know how to put these two newly acquired talents together unless you show him. In other words, he will be concentrating so hard on following a fast calf that he is apt to completely forget the cues for the stop. What are you going to do? I have always found, even though it is terribly slow and frequently boring, that the best results come from roping really slow calves, animals that just totter along, for a few weeks.

The idea is this: if you go whipping into the arena at full speed and have to use your reins to stop your horse so he will not step over the slack rope, all your careful teaching of cues will be forever forgotten. But if you take after really slow calves, you can cue your horse the way you have been doing. Slap a loop over the calf's head, toss your slack rope, shift your weight, brace yourself with your left hand on

Many-times president of the Rodeo Cowboys Association, Dale Smith, has always roped on top horseflesh, mainly because he knows how to train a horse and keep him trained.

the neck and your right hand on the horn, and get down. If the horse fails to recognize the stop cue, even while roping a slow calf, you can jerk the reins as you get off or at the time you hit the ground. But I do not think this will be necessary if you have stuck with those slow-geared calves.

After your horse is working well at a lope and controlled gallop, you can bring in some faster calves, or you can send your roping pony to a trainer, depending on how proficient you are at training or how badly you want to rope fast calves. If you have a hankering to be a professional roper, you will be pitted against rodeo calves that are big, tough, and rapid. If your bent is more toward the little shows and Sunday jackpots, then you should be able to do most of the training yourself.

The difference is what professional baseball is to the sandlot variety. It all depends on how hard, how much, and how well you want to rope.

A friend of mine, who thought he was a pretty fair roper, once got aboard a professional calf roper's horse for a practice session. Out of the chute came the calf. In a few sod-pounding strides the horse was on top of the calf and itching to stop. But our friend was taking a lot more time in throwing than the horse was accustomed to. In fact he took so much time that this old pony could not stand it any longer. He dug in with all four feet and came to a smashing stop. My friend, to his everlasting embarrassment, was catapulted right onto the horse's neck and then to the ground. Well, there are more ropers who rope just for the sport of it than there are consistent money-winners.

The point is that a fellow can have a good time training his own horses. They may be far from the world's best but they will do nicely for what he wants. When a pretty good roper, who is also a pretty good horseman, finishes a year or so of steady training, his prospect should be a polished performer. Here is what the well-trained rope horse should be able to do:

He should be able to score a calf in the box without excessive excitement or jumping around. He should never rear. Whether the barrier cord is released automatically or by hand, the rope horse should stand alert or even back down against the boards at the rear of the box. Some horses actually squat down, anticipating the cue of the roper. And the cue is usually a jab of the spurs as the roper rises forward in the saddle.

A perfect scoring horse is one that will not move until he receives the roper's cue. A perfect score, one that evokes the "Just right!" cry from the roper's buddies, happens when horse and rider reach the barrier a split second before it is released.

Now, with earth-eating strides, the rope horse overtakes the calf in

The New Mexico roper Jack Shaw throws his weight against the rope, simulating the pull of a calf, as he schools his horse to keep a taut rope.

the quickest possible way, cutting in here and turning fast there if the calf is on an erratic course. The top rope horse should be fast and have a quick change of leads. He should come up on the calf breathing fire, but then he must rate the speed of the calf with his own speed. Some ropers—most ropers—throw the second they get within reach. Others like to lie in back of the calf a moment and then throw. In this case, the horse must not run over the calf or must not overanticipate the time to stop—remember my friend's predicament—but must glide along in perfect position for the roper to throw whenever he is ready. This is called trailing or tracking cattle and most ropers will do it when they are way ahead in the average and are after their last calf. They are willing to sacrifice speed for accuracy and a dead-sure catch.

Mention should be made of that famous old rope horse, Baldy, who was so noted for his hard, clod-scattering stop. Old Baldy had another claim to fame in the arena: the way he overtook stock. He could really flatten out to catch a calf. He had a smooth and rapid change of leads. No calf ever left him on the outside of a turn.

From a hard run, after you have connected and pitched your slack rope away, the made rope horse—cued to stop as I have already discussed the matter—comes to a thudding halt. The desired stop is straight or "squared." There are many photographs of horses stopping in such a disfigured way that if they were drawn that way by an illustrator, you would swear that a horse could not get into such a position. The most common bad stop is the "corkscrew" stop, with the horse stopping in a twisted fashion, his front feet off to one side and his hind feet to the other.

It is not that a horse cannot come to a terrific whoa in this shape, but it makes dismounting just that more difficult. Now consider the horse that stops directly behind a calf, with his hind legs dug in straight beneath his body. This is the desired stop, the easiest and most convenient for the rider. In this respect, remember to rope your calf when it is running straight. No loops on the turns, unless you have got to go for day money and must risk a badly positioned throw.

The absolutely perfect stop, if you could see it from a point directly above the action, would take place in a long, very thin rectangle. The calf would be jerked back as the rope snapped taut, and there would be a straight line, from the root of the horse's tail to the root of the calf's tail, through the center of the rectangle. You can put such a stop on your pony if you keep off his mouth. Cue him, as I have discussed, by weight and hands—not by pulling on the reins.

25
Backyard Breaking and Training

My first horse of any account—and by that I mean a registered Quarter Horse—was a chestnut two-year-old named Apache Kid. I was just fourteen years old when I started breaking him, with the help of a fine old cowboy, the late Berry Gardner. In fact, Berry had sold me the colt, so he had a special interest in the finished product. He was not going to let me make a mess out of this one, who was by the Quarter Horse stallion, Lucky, a son of Ben Hur.

How I broke this colt may be of interest to readers who plan on backyard-breaking their own one of these days. There is nothing special or mysterious about the procedure. Anyone can do it, but he should possess three characteristics: a love of horseflesh, lots of patience, and a desire to see a job well done.

In the old days of the open West, cowboys would often select green horses from huge remudas, rope them on the spot, and saddle and break them in a few hours. But the next time that cowboy roped and saddled his horse, he was again prepared for a session of bucking. Some of these remuda horses never were thoroughly broken or trained, although, admittedly, some of them became top mounts. Some of them were also injured or ruined in the process of spur-of-the-moment breaking. Nowadays we have more time to make the needed effort.

To start off, the colt must be gentled so that he is tractable when it comes time to put a halter over his head. Gentleness comes quickly these days; pasture-born foals are accustomed to humans from birth. Touching, handling, patting an appealing infant foal is the beginning of the gentling process.

Even before they are weaned, at four to five months, foals can be halter broke by simply slipping on a halter and leading the foal along beside its mother. If weanlings or short yearlings are not halter broke, it may help to toss a nonslip loop over the hindquarters. Each time the youngster jerks back or fights the halter, a pull on the loop will urge him forward to escape the strange pressure around his rump. He will soon learn in perhaps a half dozen half-hour lessons to walk briskly out when pulled by the halter rope.

After the colt is halter broke, a more sophisticated hackamore is used for further training. These vary in makeup, but the most popular type is a kind of homemade rig of soft, braided rope, with a loop of soft rope for reins and a twenty-foot lead rope. Most of these advanced breaking hackamores are connected to a bosal or noseband loop by a fiador knot and, quite frankly, the only way you are going to learn how to make this rigging is to ask an old-timer to show you. Your patience in learning the art of the bosal hackamore and fiador will be well worthwhile.

Now you can lunge the colt in a large circle on the end of your twenty-foot rope, teaching him to obey the command "whoa!" And during the lunging periods, either right afterward or before, take an old saddle blanket and begin flopping it all over his rump and back and underneath his belly. When he has accepted the blanket, walk the colt around with the blanket on his back and withers.

The next step, of course, is to saddle the colt. If you are fortunate you can probably manage with the colt tied to a post, or hobbled in front, or with a hind leg drawn up under the belly. Remember to take it easy. Do not scare the colt; do not let the colt panic.

If you should be working with a particularly headstrong, excitable youngster—Apache Kid was like this—then you need the help of an able hand on a placid horse. So let me return to Apache Kid and my friend, Berry Gardner, who taught me how to break horses.

When Apache was just a little under twenty-four months, I put the saddle on him. He was fairly gentle and halter broke but he did not like that saddle one bit. I worked on the colt for several days, with Berry on a big, docile dun gelding snubbing Apache Kid down close in so that he could not duck his head and break in two bucking. At last I got the saddle on, cinched it down neat and snug, and then Berry took the colt for a long lope to acquaint him with the squeaking and creaking of leather and the bouncing of the stirrups. After a couple of weeks of this, I eased aboard. When I did cautiously step into the near side stirrup and swung my leg over, finding the offside stirrup, Apache started forward with a jump. But snubbed down as he was, he had no place to go. That jump was the only sort of pitch he ever tried to make.

A simple twist hobble can be used to saddle a young horse, even to mount him for the first few times. *Courtesy Jean D. Porter.*

Quietly ease into the saddle on a young horse in training. The basic hackamore bosal rig is shown with the loop of reins and the longer lead line tied to the saddle. *Courtesy Jean D. Porter.*

One of the reasons why the Binford Ranch of Wildorado, Texas, has such well-mannered horses is because they are properly broke and trained. Here, Nancy Binford rides a young horse in a bosal hackamore.

After another couple of weeks walking, trotting, and loping at the side of the big dun (I had the reins while Berry took the lead line), Berry said: "He's broke, Willard. He's a good horse now and won't give you any trouble. But ride him and work him—that's what a Quarter Horse is for. Don't just feed him and look at him."

And Apache was a good horse, too. I put a good rein on him in a neighbor's circular breaking corral and later took him into some sandy washes and big open fields. When he was close to three years old I started him out on slow calves, and in six months time I was winning a few dollars at some punkin' rollin' rodeos.

In all the many nuances of breaking and training Quarter Horses, here are some main points to remember:

Do not lose your temper. Some colts or fillies can be very frustrating, but to accomplish your goal you must be in control at all times. Be firm; show the colt who is master. But never beat a young horse from anger or loss of objectivity (see Chapter 7).

Be sure that your equipment—saddle, halter, bosal, ropes, and lines— is in good shape and of sufficient strength to handle the job.

If you get into a jam, if you feel for any reason that what you are doing may be wrong, or if you sense that the colt has the edge, by all means go to a professional trainer for advice. There are hundreds of trainers today all over the country.

Be sure to use ropes and lines that will not burn or scrape the young horse should he throw an unexpected wingding. Soft cotton or soft synthetics should be used for hobbling, tying up a hind foot, and for reins and lead lines on the bosal hackamore.

Do not overwork a young horse. Even though the trend today is toward younger horses on the track and in the arena, many horses break down under heavier training than they are physically equipped to handle. In the old days, a top rope horse or cutting horse was not considered really good until he had some age on him. I would say never extend a horse in an arena until he is over three years old.

Do not put severe bits into a young horse's mouth. Start with a training snaffle and use it for several months in conjunction with the hackamore. Then use it alone after you remove the hackamore. Next you can go to one of a number of different style curb bits.

Be sure not to sore a young horse's back. Use plenty of padding in the form of blankets and cushioning between the saddle's mohair and the horse's natural hair. A saddle that fits is also very important.

In this day and age there is no reason why a young horse should buck at all. But in the various stages of training he needs room to move forward. Snubbed down by a cowboy on another horse, the combination of which acts as a pivot, the young horse will merely move in a circle.

26
Kids and Quarter Horses

I once had a Quarter Horse called Hot Rod. Kids broke him in Oklahoma, where I bought him, and at least two family's children, including mine, rode him for a dozen or more years in Arizona. He was a great horse because he *was* a kid's horse in every sense of the word.

But let me tell you what this pair of knowledgeable trainers, Casey and Blair Darnell of Sandoval, New Mexico, have to say about youngsters and horses together:

CASEY: You don't want to start children out too young, because they're not physically able to do much and you've got to be so careful with them. If you ever get one really scared, it will ruin him and you'll lose him. You're better off if you wait until a kid's strong enough to ride and take the initiative on a horse. Then they learn faster and easier. A good starting age is five or six.

BLAIR: Each kid is different. Some are independent and strong-willed at six, with a real motivation to get started riding. Then you have some children at nine who are still very shy and inhibited. Riding is a good way to bring them out a little more. They are physically able to handle a horse, but mentally they are just becoming adjusted to the idea of becoming independent on a horse. Such a child, at six, wouldn't be ready at all. So it's hard to put your finger on a proper age to start them. A lot of factors are involved. What horses are available? How much money, time, and effort does the parent want to contribute? Does the child own his own horse? Where is the horse to be boarded?

Casey Darnell, expert horse breeder, trainer, and show judge of Sandoval, New Mexico, watches one of his junior misses take her horse through the paces.

CASEY: You've got to start those kids on the gentlest horses you can find. All those kids are scared when they start riding. They probably won't tell you they're scared, but they are. So the first few lessons this kid has, he's got to get enough confidence in himself—and the horse—to know that he can ride the horse. So you want a horse that will do nothing, just walk along. They have to be good and gentle and dependable.

BLAIR: And those are worth a million.

CASEY: They're really not worth much to look at, but Blair's right . . . they are worth a million dollars to a kid trying to get his courage up on top of one.

BLAIR: We started Chris [one of the Darnell children] on Roany Good Pony, and she was a dandy, gentle little horse. Actually, Chris rode in the saddle with her father first, and this, I think, helps a child develop a genuine enthusiasm for riding.

CASEY: And she wanted to get out of the arena pretty soon, too. An arena's fine for a while. But horses continually in an arena will get stale and sour, and so will kids. In order to keep them interested, you have to do different things. We find that our horses will go better out on a trail away from the arena. Just like a trail ride, the horses will follow one another. In an arena you're very much limited to what you can do, unless a kid can really ride well. About all a beginner can do in an arena is learn to walk and trot and lope. That takes quite a little time, but as soon as he learns that, you've got to do something else. Try to keep the whole thing interesting and challenging for him.

BLAIR: I think training a kid to ride is much like breaking and training a young horse. You need a lot of miles to make a good horse and you need a lot of miles to make a good rider. They should be chaperoned or supervised to start with, taught good habits, and then they'll end up being able to handle a good horse later on.

CASEY: As soon as they have enough confidence in their ability to ride and handle the horse, you should turn them loose out of the arena. But remember, you should know that they are able to ride this horse. It's kind of like a first drive in a car or the first solo in an airplane. Send a couple of kids off together on a pair of those million-dollar horses for their first ride. I don't think kids should go out their first time or two by themselves. Send them out with another kid who can ride, somebody who can keep them out of trouble. Or you can send the younger ones with the older kids.

BLAIR: Once in a while one or two of them are going to have some bad experiences and have to walk home. They're going to tie the horses up and have the reins busted, or they're going to be shaken off. There are always those kids who think they can do it before they are ready to, and you just have to let them learn. You don't want to dwell on danger too much, but the child must learn that he has a responsibility both to himself and his horse to avoid situations that could become dangerous. You tell them reasons for doing and not doing certain things. I think Casey's way has certainly been very good. He puts them up there and starts them riding. He doesn't pussy-foot around. He gets them into the saddle and then they automatically learn the right way to start.

CASEY: When I first start a bunch of kids, I don't tell them that riding a horse is dangerous. I try to build their confidence in themselves, their horses, and their ability to ride. This way, you don't have any—or many—problems later on. Don't dwell on how they might get hurt, because, gee whiz, a kid might get hurt any place . . . charging down the road on a bicycle. Sooner or later, he's going to learn about his horse and he's going to learn that there are dangers and that if a horse steps on his toe, it hurts.

BLAIR: I guess I'm the cautious one in the family and I get upset when Casey leaves me to mount the kids without telling me who has been riding what. I think it's very important to pay close attention to the horse and child and to move them around and rotate them, but not to overmount them. Casey's never had a wreck with a child, never, but I have . . . and I'm the one who's super cautious. And yet I'm the one who's lost a kid or two in the arroyo.

CASEY: But you put them right back in the saddle and made them ride their horses back home.

Casey Darnell tosses a keen and critical eye on a pair of youngsters learning the fundamentals about riding.

BLAIR: I didn't let them walk home, that's for sure. But you should be certain it's the kid's fault and not the horse's. Once or twice with our own children, the horses have been pretty high, wanting to run and bolt home. Our own children were overmounted. So I took them off and let them ride back with me, because I didn't think the horse was safe to ride back. You have to make sure why the child fell off. Did the horse feel good and hump just a little? Did the child lose his balance? If that happened you put the youngster back up. But if it's clearly the horse's fault, that's what we call being overmounted, and you've made a mistake to begin with and you should let the child ride home with you.

CASEY: Riding, to most parents, is a way to get a kid past a certain stage. And if they can get the kid past this stage, their mission is accomplished. There are some kids that will go on . . . and girls in particular will ride on until they get through high school or college. Boys are apt to quit on you about the time they go to high school, when they start football or baseball or track or some other activity that's more readily available to them. Of course, some boys, and many more girls, become accomplished riders and will want to go on to the horse shows. These mature boys and girls get a great satisfaction out of being able to make a horse do what they want him to do.

BLAIR: From the modern girl's viewpoint—and my own from years past—they like to go through a period of wearing jeans and boots and playing cowgirl and getting a horse, if they can.

CASEY: To go back to when they're little kids again, I think they learn how to dress and ride from watching each other. I think the younger ones learn as much—or more maybe—from the older riders as they do from the instructor. So I think it's better to throw boys and girls together in beginners' riding classes. The same with age. We always try to get a few older kids to ride with the younger ones. Mix age groups up.

BLAIR: The ideal class consists of about a half a dozen or eight kids. And it might be an hour or more in length. An hour and a half isn't too long when children are interested in what they're doing. This might include a fifteen-minute warming up period, and there's always the cooling down period, especially after they've been out on the trail. Usually each horse can work hard ten or fifteen minutes. And then their riders hold them in and wait and watch the others, which is part

Darnell discusses a problem with one of his young charges learning riding at the veteran horseman's place at Sandoval, New Mexico.

of the learning, as Casey said. Occasionally you will find a student that needs a lot of concentrated work and some pretty intense attention. But for the most part, they learn better in a group that contains both beginners and more experienced riders. Now also, if these children are really interested they will be helped by the more advanced kids along horse husbandry lines and caring for their saddles and bridles.

CASEY: As far as learning the parts of the horse and how to care for a horse and equipment, the 4-H Club has a good program. They teach the kids these things from the book, and the kids, I think, learn easier from the pictures than they can from an instructor, whose main function, after all, is to teach riding. It's important they learn these things, but of most importance is learning to ride well.

BLAIR: Generally the kids that are fond of horses and who are really doing well at the shows come from one- or two-child families. This tells you quite a bit about the horse business. It means the family can afford a top horse and top equipment for their child or just a pair of children. It's great for those families and their child or pair of children, but I think it gives an unrealistic picture of horses and kids. If there are four or five kids in a family there is no way that family can send their kids first class to the horse shows. But these children can still have a real interest in riding and it's perfectly possible for these multi-children families to have fun horseback riding. And they don't have to be involved in the horse show scene. I think that perhaps we dwell too heavily on the horse show scene because there is more glamour to it than just riding. But it's unrealistic. Very few families can afford to haul four separate registered Quarter Horses to a youth show, or to a regular show, and outfit four kids . . . and not belong to a very special group of people. So I don't think that horse showing is the ultimate goal, even though it's very nice for those who can afford it. We don't emphasize horse shows when we teach riding. First of all, we are teaching them to ride a horse and to have fun doing it. A lot of people think that kids are learning to ride to go to the shows. But that's just one area for a group of people. Some of our students may never own a horse. But later on, if they want advice, they'll ask us questions and maybe we can help them make up their minds about different kinds of horses. Some place in their training they should ride some horse of good breeding, one that is willing.

CASEY: But first, as we said, you have to put the kid on a gentle horse that he can control. Now as the kid learns to ride, what he wants to do, I think, will dictate what kind of a horse he has to have. And the conditions he wants to ride under, and how much he can afford to pay for a horse, have a lot to do with what he'll get. Kids have ways of getting what they want through life and there are a lot of people, including their families, who will help them. If kids decide they want something, and want it bad enough to go out and work for it, what they can get is unlimited. One of the things they can get is a good horse. Like roping. I think if a kid gets to the point where he wants to rope—say fourteen years old—and he's developed himself on an old horse and knows he's getting pretty good, then he'll get the money somehow to buy himself a top horse. Same thing with horse shows. If he wants to show horses bad enough and he goes to the shows and sees what kinds of horses the kids are winning on, then that's the kind of a horse he knows he has to have . . . if he's going to try to beat them. So it all depends on what a kid is going to do with a horse. If he's satisfied with a lazy old trail horse, fine. As Blair said, he doesn't have to go the horse show route. But if he does want to show horses, or rope, or cut . . . then he's got to go to a better, breedier animal. Look at barrel racing, for instance. You've got to have a really top horse with speed.

BLAIR: It would certainly help all horse trainers and all instructors—people in a position to sell a horse—to do it with a great deal of forethought. Because to give bad advice is much worse than giving no advice. In trying to sell a horse to a family, when there is some doubt in the seller's mind as to how suitable the horse is to the family, is a very bad thing to do. And unfortunately a lot of professional horse people don't consider all aspects of a sale. For instance, maybe it's the worst thing in the world for a three-child family to get a two-thousand-dollar horse for one of the children. We've seen several families bite the dirt. One family quit horses completely and has a very bad feeling about horse people and the horse business. This sort of thing puts pressure on the professional horseman to give his best and his honest recommendations to families that are in the process of buying better-grade horses for the children.

CASEY: Let me add a little something here. The first cost in one of those horses is the cheapest. The everyday upkeep of the horse is the most expensive. It's going to cost a family two or three dollars a day, at least, to maintain this horse. All this includes board, feed, shoeing, veterinary bills, and clothes and tack for the kid. Now it's hard for a father, the head of the family, to really know if his kid is ready for an expensive horse. He'll have to depend on suggestions from the instructor. And the kid will help, too, if he's really serious about riding.

27
A Strong Incentive for
Youth Participation

Except for the previous chapter, in which the Darnells discuss very small children and horses, I have aimed most of my remarks toward adults. However, the AQHA has a program for juniors (see Introduction) that is a strong incentive to participate in Quarter Horse doings. It is simply called Youth Activities and, according to the association, the AQHA is "the first horse-breed organization to sponsor a Youth Activities program wherein boys and girls 18 years of age and under may compete apart from adults for handsome, costly awards and public acclaim."

The AQHA still further advances the roll of competing youngsters by letting them manage their own association within the parent association. It is called the American Junior Quarter Horse Association— for "boys and girls 18 years of age and under who are members of any recognized state junior Quarter Horse association."

But boys and girls who already own registered Quarter Horses need not belong to the AJQHA or any other junior group to participate in Youth Activity classes.

The objectives and purposes of the AJQHA, as defined by the parent association, are as follows:

• To improve and promote the American Quarter Horse breed.
• To improve and develop the capabilities of youth individually and collectively through group participation in the breeding, raising, and exhibition of registered Quarter Horses.

Many schools and communities encourage the juniors in rodeo and horse shows. Scooter Fries, as far back as 1948, was awarded a Quarter Horse colt for being the champion high school roper of Texas. *Courtesy Virgil Minear.*

● To develop and improve scholarship, leadership, and community interest and participation of young horsemen.

● To encourage high moral character, sportsmanship, and clean living among all its members.

● To enable junior members to work in conjunction with the American Quarter Horse Association's Youth Activities committee.

● To create, foster, and assist subsidiary state junior associations comprised of members of the American Junior Quarter Horse Association.

● To acquaint junior members and associations with the functions and services of the American Quarter Horse Association.

Membership fee in the American Junior Quarter Horse Association is one dollar annually, to be collected by state Junior Quarter Horse Associations.

It is interesting to note that the AQHA is the only horse breed association mentioned on the inside front page of *Horses and Horsemanship*, a publication of the 4-H Horsemanship Program. The paragraph reads: "The Horse Publication Series was prepared by the Federal and State Extension Services in cooperation with the National 4-H Service Committee and the American Quarter Horse Association, for use by the Cooperative Extension Services in connection with the 4-H Horse Project."

In the past few years, kids that might have turned to cattle or sheep or even another breed of horse are going all out for Quarter Horses for their 4-H projects. So the AQHA is reciprocating by making its breed of horse as attractive as possible.

A special event in which the Quarter Horse stars is the annual National Youth Horse Congress, last held in Dallas, Texas. Jammed into this six-day extravaganza are 4-H Club horse shows, all-breed shows, seminars, discussions, demonstrations and clinics, and an AQHA-approved all-youth Quarter Horse show.

Classes at each NYH Congress include halter, western pleasure, western horsemanship, reining, barrel running, pole bending, cutting, breakaway roping, hunt seat equitation, saddle seat equitation, jumping, and working hunter.

Another sport that increases enjoyment of Quarter Horses for young people in a slightly higher age bracket is college rodeo. The National Intercollegiate Rodeo Association reports that "about 3,000 students go out for rodeo each year." The NIRA is divided into eight regions which hold fourteen to twenty rodeos every year.

Contests for men include bareback bronc riding, saddle bronc riding, steer wrestling, bull riding, calf roping, and team roping. Contests for women are barrel running, goat tying, and ribbon roping.

If memory serves me, the University of Arizona at Tucson, around 1940, was the first such school to hold a rodeo among its students. In following years, other schools and colleges were invited to compete, and the student cowboy was created on an intercollegiate basis.

Several schools exist around the country that cater to the junior horseman and horsewoman. Probably the best known is Tommy Manion's Youth Activities School, located at the Illinois State fairgrounds in Springfield. Manion usually conducts his schools, in July of each year, in a pair of sessions: one for thirteen-year-olds and under and one for fourteen-year-olds and over.

Classes offered are instruction in horsemanship and showing at halter, western pleasure, reining, and English pleasure. Manion makes his school exciting and entertaining. He offers weekly prizes (saddles, boots, etc.) for students showing the most aptitude. Also, special attractions may include prominent guest speakers from the world of Quarter Horses, AQHA and other special films from the files of pro-

Poco Tinto Dolly, 1971 Champion Western Riding Horse owned by Willow Brook Farms in Pennsylvania, is being ridden here by Donna Anthony.

fessional trainers, style shows, and guest instructors. In 1971, a total of eighty-seven juniors from seventeen states and Canada attended the school.

All this fuss concerning our children's interest in Quarter Horses makes sense. In the first place today's juniors will soon be tomorrow's adults—so we might as well see to it that they are learning the right things about horses and, more particularly, about Quarter Horses. Moreover, with a solid base of youth interest in Quarter Horses, the industry is assured of a self-perpetuating and healthy future—from generation to generation.

Horses, too, provide a means of personal recognition, something that most young people yearn for and deserve. To award the deserving, the AQHA has formulated an annual Honor Roll Trophy in each of the Youth Activity events, and an All-Around Trophy to the youth who earns the most points with one horse in both the halter and performance classes.

The year-end Honor Roll Awards will be made in the following events: halter mare, halter gelding, showmanship at halter, western pleasure, cutting, reining, barrel racing, calf roping, breakaway roping, western riding, trail class, stake race, pole bending, western horsemanship, jumping, working cowhorse, working hunter, and English pleasure.

In order to be eligible for a special year-end, all-around performance trophy, a junior contestant must compete in at least three approved youth performance events, which include most of those events just mentioned.

The AQHA, as you can see, is strongly behind the equine-oriented youth of the nation. The association recommends that show managements provide a youth division for junior exhibitors. Junior shows, however, will be approved by the AQHA separately or in conjunction with adult shows.

1971 Youth Honor Roll

MARES   (Points)
1. Danny Due, Splash Bar Maid, Groveton, Texas............129
2. Sabrina Graham, Sabrina Lee, Rocheport, Missouri...........114
3. Bob Pentzien, Golden Lea Miss, Omaha, Nebraska........ 62

GELDINGS
1. Vicki Tompkins, Tuff Joe Reed, Des Moines, Iowa...........180
2. Jimmy Palmer, Denver Jack, Venetia, Pennsylvania.........127
3. Kathy Kraus, Barjay Dude, Quincy, Illinois............ 71

SHOWMANSHIP
1. Kathy Kraus, Barjay Dude, Quincy, Illinois 246
2. Linda Fitterling, Roca Girl, South Bend, Indiana 167
3. Sabrina Graham, Sabrina Lee, Rocheport, Missouri 165

WESTERN PLEASURE
1. Sabrina Graham, Sabrina Lee, Rocheport, Missouri 410
2. Kathy Kraus, Barjay Dude, Quincy, Illinois 324
3. Marty Heberding, King's Marion, Galena, Ohio 194

CUTTING
1. Warren Patrick, Jr., You Catch Him, Tallulah, Louisiana 15
2. Alice Vickers, Hollywood Josie, Pascagoula, Mississippi 10

REINING
1. George Williams, Snoopy Tag, Vero Beach, Florida 65
2. Linda Fitterling, Roca Girl, South Bend, Indiana 56
3. Carolyn Potter, Sissy Pete, Northport, New York 33

BARREL RACING
1. Scott Van Klompenberg, Dilly's Copper, Hudsonville, Michigan 36
2. Prudie Casselman, Okie Flyer, Midland, Texas 30
3. Kay Carlton, Jennifer Reed, Anadarko, Oklahoma 21

WESTERN RIDING
1. Monica Hemberger, Carla's Poco, New Berlin, Illinois 34
2. Linda Fitterling, Roca Girl, South Bend, Indiana 18
3. Nina Stewart, Poco Suggie Buck, Dallas, Texas 17

TRAIL CLASS
1. Susan Bennett, Parlay Bar, Thompson, Connecticut 23
2. Laura Stroh, Jade Island, Gig Harbor, Washington 21
3. Laura Hall, Tabano Dave, Greensboro, North Carolina 18

POLE BENDING
1. Catherine Ann Brown, Wimpy's Star Jet, Laurel, Mississippi 23
2. Nonie Casselman, Okie Flyer, Midland, Texas 15
3. Terry Messenger, Mandan's Feather, Oklahoma City, Oklahoma 14

WESTERN HORSEMANSHIP
1. Linda Fitterling, Roca Girl, South Bend, Indiana 235
2. Marty Heberding, King's Marion, Galena, Ohio 201
3. Kathy Kraus, Barjay Dude, Quincy, Illinois 193

ENGLISH PLEASURE
1. Kathy Kraus, Barjay Dude, Quincy, Illinois 102
2. Marty Heberding, King's Marion, Galena, Ohio 49
3. Linda Fitterling, Roca Girl, South Bend, Indiana 48
   Sabrina Graham, Sabrina Lee, Rocheport, Missouri 48

All Around

1. Kathy Kraus, Barjay Dude, Quincy, Illinois 936
2. Sabrina Graham, Sabrina Lee, Rocheport, Missouri 870
3. Linda Fitterling, Roca Girl, South Bend, Indiana 723
4. Gigi Challas, Izzy's Jacket, Calumet City, Illinois 425
5. Kathy Kirsch, El Skip, Sturgis, Michigan 262
6. Walter B. Williams, III, Aledo Rita Bar, Milledgeville, Georgia 232
7. Kim Bird, Hay Valley Pat, Detroit, Michigan 214
8. Marilyn Norris, Ruby Red Miller, Dallas, Texas 211
9. Vicki Tompkins, Tuff Joe Reed, Des Moines, Iowa 186
10. Susan Brooks, My Rawhide, Santa Ana, California 185

Youth Activity Honor Roll

All Around Champion

1970	Dianne Sapp, Miss Baleo	529
1969	Sandy Warren, Edred B Maid	381
1968	Sue Boland, Yeller Hi Life	206½
1967	Rick Skelly, Mano's Billy Van	212½
1966	Nancy Edwards, Dooley Dan	166

Champion Mare

1970	Nancy Ricards, She's a Shiny	67
1969	Tom Forst, Desto Bar	67
1968	Sue Boland, Champ's Tica	32
1967	Nancy Neher, Bobbibar Bob	58
1966	Tim Walker, Frosty Money	19

Champion Gelding

1970	Jimmy Palmer, Denver Jack	87
1969	Marilyn Norris, Dun King Leo	75
1968	Debby Brehm, Johnny Pat Star	66
1967	Michael Allen, Bell Man	44
1966	Kathy Gunson, Scamp's Nugget	17

28
Roundup of Quarter Horse Information

In addition to the parent Quarter Horse association, the AQHA, and its many affiliates in the United States, there are three countries that boast of groups dedicated to the advancement of this breed. They are in Australia, Canada, and Mexico and here are the names and addresses of the groups:

Australian Quarter Horse Association. Secretary: Royal Agricultural Society of New South Wales, Box 4317, G. P. O., Sydney, New South Wales, 2001 Australia.

Canadian Quarter Horse Association. Secretary: A. P. Bowsher, R. R. 8, Calgary, Alberta, Canada.

Associacion Mexicana Cuarto de Milla. Secretary: Manuel Mondragon H., Insurgentes Sur 1180–502, Mexico 12, D. F., Mexico.

● All of us who have owned, ridden, bred, or simply admired Quarter Horses have tried, at one time or another, to visualize our ideal horse. It is easy to picture an ideal in the mind's eye, but it is far from easy to find or produce that ideal. Most horsemen, I think, tend to be overly critical of their own horse-breeding efforts, their own operations. And this attitude is a good thing, for it stimulates a still greater interest in the search for the ideal, or near-ideal type.

● Roy Savage, former Oklahoma rodeo roper and currently a Quarter Horse breeder and trainer, recently told me: "I would rather raise one good foal than a dozen average ones. Always remember, in this business it costs no more to raise and feed a good horse than it does a poor one. A newcomer to the business should learn the basics of what constitutes a sound, well-conformed Quarter Horse. He should always be able to criticize his horses and know their faults better than anyone else."

• Locations of the annual AQHA conventions: 1940–49, Fort Worth, Texas; 1950, Amarillo, Texas; 1951, Colorado Springs, Colorado; 1952, College Station, Texas; 1953, Tucson, Arizona; 1954, Albuquerque, New Mexico; 1955, Long Beach, California; 1956, Houston, Texas; 1957, Oklahoma City, Oklahoma; 1958, Tucson, Arizona; 1959, Fort Worth, Texas; 1960, Amarillo, Texas; 1961, Denver, Colorado; 1962, Long Beach, California; 1963, Tulsa, Oklahoma; 1964, Phoenix, Arizona; 1965, Dallas, Texas; 1966, Cincinnati, Ohio; 1967, New Orleans, Louisiana; 1968, Las Vegas, Nevada; 1969, Fort Worth, Texas; 1970, San Francisco, California; 1971, Mexico City, Mexico; 1972, Kansas City, Missouri; 1973, Dallas, Texas; 1974, Honolulu, Hawaii.

• Ask the average rider which is the best saddle horse, and he is bound to put a good word in for the Quarter Horse, along with the Standardbred and Morgan. Ask the racehorse man which is the fastest short-distance sprinter, and nine times out of ten he will say the Quarter Horse. Ask the cowboy which is the best cow pony, and ninety-nine out of one hundred times he will say the Quarter Horse. Ask anyone which is the best-looking horse in America today, and, I think, the answer will usually be the Quarter Horse.

World's Champion Quarter Running Horses

1971	Charger Bar, b. m. 68 by Tiny Charger
1970	Kaweah Bar, pal. g. 66 by Alamitos Bar
1969	Easy Jet, ch. c. 67 by Jet Deck
1968	Kaweah Bar, pal. h. 66 by Alamitos Bar
1967	Laico Bird, br. m. 65 by Good Bird (TB)
1966	(No award)
1965	Go Josie Go, s. m. 62 by Go Man Go
1964	Goetta, b. m. 61 by Go Man Go
1963	Jet Deck, b. h. 60 by Moon Deck
1962	No Butt, b. m. 55 by Joe Less
1961	Pap, ch. g. 54 by Papitas
1960	Vandy's Flash, ch. g. 54 by Vandy
1959	(No award)
1958	Mr. Bar None, ch. h. 55 by Three Bars (TB)
1957	Go Man Go, ro. h. 53 by Top Deck (TB)
1956	Go Man Go, ro. h. 53 by Top Deck (TB)
1955	Go Man Go, ro. h. 53 by Top Deck (TB)
1954	Josie's Bar, ch. m. 51 by Three Bars (TB)
1953	Miss Meyers, ch. m. 49 by Leo

1952   Johnny Dial, br. h. 48 by Depth Charge (TB)
1951   Monita, ch. m. 47 by Joe Moore
         Maddon's Bright Eyes, b. m. 46 by Gold Mount
1950   Blob, Jr., ch. h. 47 by Blob (TB)

● In breeding Quarter Horses today, as in the past, horsemen are looking for the best possible results. To get these results—or at least to try to get them—they are paying very strict attention to bloodlines. Of course conformation and performance count, too, but horsemen are discovering that it is not by accident that the names of many famous old Quarter Horses appear again and again in the pedigrees of today's living horses.

AQHA Supreme Champions

The official handbook of the AQHA states: "The title 'AQHA Supreme Champion' will be awarded to any stallion, mare, or gelding which has been issued a numbered registration certificate by the American Quarter Horse Association . . . [and] meets the following requirements: A. Has earned two official Speed Index Ratings at 90 or higher (AAA); B. Has been named Grand Champion at a minimum of two approved A shows under two different judges; C. Has won a total of forty (40) or more points in recognized halter and performance classes at A shows approved by the Association or in races recognized by the Association. . . ." Here they are through 1971:

Astro Deck, s. h. 62, Top Deck (TB)–Flo St. Jo, owned by Clary Spencer, Edmond, Oklahoma; bred by Robert Sukman, Edmond, Oklahoma.

Back Stretch, b. h. 61, Diamond 2 Bar–Annette Kay, owned by Morley Quarter Horse Ranch, Yakima, Washington; bred by J. Ralph Bell, Visalia, California.

Bar Money, ch. h. 60, Three Bars (TB)–Miss Ruby, owned by J. Thomas Heckel, Jr., St. Louis Missouri; bred by Walter Merrick, Sayre, Oklahoma.

Cat's Cue Bar, ch. g. 61, Catechu–Chicabar Doll, owned by LeRoy S. and/or Barbara McCay, Eugene, Oregon; bred by Homer D. Sims, Lebanon, Oregon.

Desto Bar, ch. m. 63, Nug Bar–Billie Texas, owned by Mr. or Mrs. R. C. Johns, Phoenix, Arizona; bred by Bert J. Montgomery, Modesto, California.

Diamond Dividend, blk. h. 65, Senor Campos–King's Kay, owned by Mrs. Alma V. Tamborello, Burkeville, Texas; bred by Mrs. P. C. DePew, Grapevine, Texas.

Diamond Duro, blk. h. 65, Diamond Charge–Missy Bar Leo, owned by Eddie and Connie Crowell, West Dennis, Massachusetts; bred by Bob Wilkinson, Canyon, Texas.

Enhanced, b. h. 61, J B King–Nancy Hance, bred and owned by Jay Parsons, Cody, Wyoming.

Fairbars, ch. h. 61, Three Bars (TB)–Lady Fairfax, owned by Grafton Moore, Holly, Michigan; bred by Quincy Farms, Denver, Colorado.

Goodbye Sam, d. h. 64, Fairfax Joe–Maudie Leo, owned by L. M. Patterson and George H. Price, Fairview, Tennessee; bred by Lester Williams, Fairfax, Oklahoma.

Jetaway Reed, s. h. 64, Depth Bars–Jo Van Reed, bred and owned by A. W. Holiday, Stillwater, Oklahoma.

Kid Meyers, s. h. 63, Three Bars (TB)–Miss Meyers, bred and owned by A. B. Green, Purcell, Oklahoma.

Leo Maudie, b. h. 61, Leo–Maudie Williams, owned by Richard C. or Josephine I. Waldner, Brookings, South Dakota; bred by L. E. Williams, Fairfax, Oklahoma.

Lightning Rey, s. h. 58, Lightning Bar–Reina Rey, owned by American Breeders Service, Inc., De Forest, Wisconsin; bred by John P. and Margaret Ann Rubel, Seligman, Arizona.

Mach I, pal. h. 60, Junior Reed–Spanish Joy, owned by L. L. and Linda Pritchett, Cottonwood, California; bred by Elna McKee, Norwood, Colorado.

Milk River, ch. h. 61, Custus Rastus–Leolib, owned by James D. Hively, Kennewick, Washington; bred by L. L. Tuck, Littleton, Colorado.

Miss Roy Deck, s. m. 63, Roy Deck–Bar Y Fancy, owned by James R. Brennan and John J. O'Brien, Skokie, Illinois; bred by Driggers Land and Cattle Company, Santa Rosa, New Mexico.

My Stormy Boy, br. h. 58, They Say (TB)–Annver, owned by Bob and/or Linda Hamilton, Paradise Valley, Arizona; bred by J. A. Hamilton, Chandler, Arizona.

● Hugh Bennett, Quarter Horse breeder from Colorado and a past AQHA president, once said: "I like a horse that can do something . . . and I try to breed 'em like that. If a horse *can't* do anything, I'll give him away. If a stud can't get what I want, I'll get rid of him, too."

● The *Official Handbook* of the AQHA, which is updated and republished on a yearly basis, reveals in the foreword: "The American Quarter Horse Association was organized in 1940 to collect, record and preserve the pedigrees of Quarter Horses. The Association also serves as an information center for its members and the general public on matters pertaining to shows, contests and projects designed to improve the breed and aid the industry."

● At last count the National Cutting Horse Association, whose members breed and use mostly Quarter Horses, had a total membership of twenty-two hundred members in forty-five states, Canada, and Australia. The NCHA has sixty-six affiliated groups. The membership consists of ranchers, farmers, businessmen, and individuals who find enjoyment in competitive cattle cutting in both large and small shows across the nation.

A pair of fast Quarter Horses trap a steer between them at the Cheyenne Frontier Days Rodeo. Dick Truitt is the 'dogger and Dave Campbell is the hazer—two of the best ever. *Courtesy DeVere Helfrich.*

Honor Roll Horses

The following horses were named champions in their respective events by the AQHA:

CUTTING (Points)

1971	Cutter's First, pal. g. 60 by Cutter Bill	48
1970	Jessie James Leo, p. h. 66 by War Bond Leo	60
1969	War Bond Leo, s. h. 63 by War Leo	81
1968	Señor George, b. h. 54 by Claude	79
1967	Heart 109, d. m. 58 by Moorhouse's Hollywood	139
1966	Marbo McCue, s. m. 60 by Gidden's Smoky	122
1965	Patty Conger, d. m. 58 by Bill Conger	139
1964	Deuce Five, s. g. 55 by Silver Wimpy	109
1963	Hoppen, b. m. 55 by Quarterback	171
1962	Cutter Bill, pal. h. 55 by Buddy Dexter	154
1961	Poco Lena, b. m. 49 by Poco Bueno	162
1960	Poco Lena, b. m. 49 by Poco Bueno	147
1959	Poco Lena, b. m. 49 by Poco Bueno	130
1958	Poco Stampede, dn. h. 52 by Poco Bueno	94
1957	Poco Stampede, dn. h. 52 by Poco Bueno	32
1956	Trinket Bennett, pal. m. 48 by Sand Bowl	33
1955	Trinket Bennett, pal. m. 48 by Sand Bowl	21
1954	Miss Texas Craft, blk. m. 49 by Double Star	115
1953	Miss Nancy Bailey, b. m. 46 by Royal King	57
1952	Miss Nancy Bailey, b. m. 46 by Royal King	31

CALF ROPING

1971	Floydada Chubby, dn. h. 57 by Chubby's Dusty	37
1970	Major Chalfant, s. g. 58 by Rawhide Hill	35
1969	Johnny Red Boy, s. h. 55 by Rusty Irish	31
1968	Pistol's Hornet, s. g. 61 by Pistol's Man	50
1967	Pistol's Hornet, s. g. 61 by Pistol's Man	58
1966	Pistol's Hornet, s. g. 61 by Pistol's Man	40
1965	Dr. Cutter, dn. h. 55 by Whizaway	44
1964	Echo Reed, b. g. 59 by Ed Echols	33
1963	Peter John, br. g. 50 by Johnny Barnes	30
1962	Rex Del Rancho, ch. h. 56 by Rey Del Rancho	27
1961	Tender Boy, s. h. 55 by Bartender	19
1960	Rondo Bill, blk. g. 55 by Baldy C	13
1959	Sonora Monkey, ch. g. 50 by Lauro	20
1958	George Dun, dn. g. 53 by Hollywood George	18
1957	George Dun, dn. g. 53 by Hollywood George	12
1956	Knocky, ch. g. 48 by King Raffles (TB)	15
1955	Jeanne's Patsy, b. m. 50 by Bert	13
1954	Pretty Boy Pokey, dn. g. 48 by Poco Bueno	12
1953	Bar V Jo B, ch. m. 45 by Buck Hancock	6
1952	Star Jack Jr., b. g. 48 by Scroggins' Little Star	11

REINING

1971	Sapphire Cody, bkn. m. 67 by Joe Cody	71
1970	Jay's Sugar Bars, s. h. 63 by Sugar Bars	91
1969	Nifty Della Bee, br. m. 65 by Nifty Bee	75
1968	Paprika Cody, s. m. 64 by Joe Cody	122

1967   Tookie's Two, pal. m. 62 by Two D Two 110
1966   Teaka Cee, b. m. 63 by Poco Do Right   87
1965   Easter Cody, d. m. 60 by Joe Cody   97
1964   Annie Blitzen, b. m. 61 by Flying Bar   67
1963   Sappho Cody, d. m. 59 by Joe Cody   75
1962   Cowboy Jim, b. g. 55 by Venture Bill   62
1961   Magnolia Dunny, dn. h. 53 by Sunup H   41
1960   Short Spark, pal. h. 56 by Shortcut   49
1959   Sonora Monkey, ch. g. 50 by Lauro   50
1958   Rondo's King, ch. h. 54 by Saltillo   27
1957   Outer's Stubby, pal. g. 52 by Baker's Oklahoma Star ...   32
1956   Knocky, ch. g. 48 by King Raffles (TB)   61
1955   Dee Gee, b. m. 45 by Bartender   26
1954   Phoebe Chess, ch. m. 48 by Eddie   12
1953   Gray Lady Burk, gr. m. 48 by Waggoner   10
1952   Sobre's Sweetie, ch. m. 49 by Sobre   6

BARREL RACING

1971   Stoner's Honey, s. m. 64 by Royal Handy   44
1970   Lucid Leo, b. g. 63 by Leo Caine   49
1969   Hillbilly King, s. g. 60 by Illini King II   69
1968   Adams' Moore, b. h. 59 by Star Bright Moore 104
1967   Mr. Kingsville, pal. h. 60 by Kingsville   70
1966   Pearl's King Leo, ch. h. 59 by Mac Lee   85
1965   King Jingles, s. h. 61 by Jim King   51
1964   Tiger Lynn, s. g. 51 by Keeno Junior   44
1963   Tiger Lynn, s. g. 51 by Keeno Junior   49
1962   Pat Dawson, pal. g. 54 by Gold King Bailey   40
1961   Pat Dawson, pal. g. 54 by Gold King Bailey   25
1960   Anadorno Peppy, ch. h. 53 by Peppy Bueno   17
1959   V's Joe Blake, b. g. 49 by Little Jodie   11
1958   Jacky's Baby, br. m. 54 by Jack Irelan   12
1957   Lady J Bailey, ch. m. 52 by Tiger Joe Bailey   5

POLE BENDING

1971   Wimpy's Star Jet, dn. g. 64 by Irby's Sandspur   27
1970   Jay Jay, s. g. 57 by Lampasas Little George   34
1969   Jay Jay, s. g. 57 by Lampasas Little George   46
1968   Jay Jay, s. g. 57 by Lampasas Little George   31
1967   Jay Jay, s. g. 57 by Lampasas Little George 24½
1966   Adams' Rocket, b. g. 59 by Star Bright Moore   17
1965   Adams' Rocket, b. g. 59 by Star Bright Moore   14
1964   Adams' Rocket, b. g. 59 by Star Bright Moore 8½
1963   Buck's Kitty, d. m. 57 by Buck Sudan 7½
1962   My Good Boy, b. g. 51 by Lobo Red 6½
1961   Buck's Lou, pal. m. 56 by Buckskin Hank 2½
       Dawson Nowata, s. g. 54 by Wimpy II 2½
       G-Fern Scat Cat, ch. h. 50 by Catechu 2½
       Midnight Bar, ch. g. 51 by Barred 2½

STEER ROPING

Year	Horse	Points
1971	Bar Fred, s. h. 64 by Fred Lowry	33
1970	Leyba Chester, p. g. 61 by Sirlette	33
1969	Leyba Chester, p. g. 61 by Sirlette	18
	Silver Son, p. h. 60 by Senator	18
1968	Leyba Chester, p. g. 61 by Sirlette	26
1967	Mr. Nimble Toes, s. g. 63 by Diamond Salute	13
	Vanguard, ch. h. 57 by Vandy	13
1966	Tender's Tonka, b. g. 62 by Tender Boy	17
	Tender Taos, b. g. 61 by Tender Boy	17
1965	Super Duper, s. g. 55 by Super Charge	12
1964	Circle Kaye, br. g. 60 by Midnight Third	5
	Mulhall Star, s. h. 58 by Guthrie Double Star	5
	Tender's Sioux, b. m. 60 by Tender Boy	5
	Arrow Ko Ko Mo, blk. h. 57 by Baldy C	5
1963	King's Cue, ch. h. 59 by King Fritz	4

WESTERN RIDING

Year	Horse	Points
1971	Poco Tinto Dolly, s. m. 65 by Poco Tinto	42
1970	King Clipper Joe, b. g. 62 by Fourble Joe	50
1969	Show Tip, s. h. 60 by Showdown	55
1968	Oscar Blob Jr., br. g. 56 by Blob Jr.	20½
1967	Toppereno, d. g. 57 by Shorty Bill	35½
1966	Cajun Springs, s. g. 62 by Cajun Creek	20½
1965	Toppereno, d. g. 57 by Shorty Bill	24½
1964	Toppereno, d. g. 57 by Shorty Bill	20½
1963	Toppereno, d. g. 57 by Shorty Bill	11
1962	Baldy Buzz, ch. h. 52 by Buzz Bomb	7½
1961	Duzer Rondo, b. g. 54 by Billy Rondo	14½
1960	Abney's Ginger, pal. m. 51 by Rattler	7½
1959	Duzer Rondo, b. g. 54 by Billy Rondo	8
1958	King Vaquero, blk. g. 53 by King's Joe Boy	26
1957	Katy Scarlet, ch. m. 52 by Snip Red	24
1956	Figa Hancock, ro. m. 51 by Grey Badger II	13
1955	Beth B, ch. m. 47 by Little King George	6
	Fancy Branch, b. m. 51 by Wimpy III	6
	Faye King, dn. m. 48 by King Gotch	6
	Little One, b. m. 51 by Bob Steel	6
1954	Beth B, ch. m. 47 by Little King George	4
1953	Whitcomb's Frogette, ch. m. 50 by Frog W	5
1952	Brown Jo Tuff, br. m. 49 by Tuffy Jo Jo	2

WORKING COWHORSE

Year	Horse	Points
1971	Dinah Solis, b. m. 64 by Solis Cogdell	20
1970	Big Sun, b. h. 66 by Eternal Sun	17
1969	Drift O Smoke, ro. m. 64 by Chipper Wood	11
1968	Justa Leo, ch. g. 63 by Otto's Jeff	8
1967	Easter Cody, d. m. 60 by Joe Cody	69
1966	Easter Cody, d. m. 60 by Joe Cody	42
1965	Semotan's Pal, pal. h. 53 by Little Cowboy	20

The Quarter Horse calmly carries Old Glory in parades and grand entries.

1964 Camelot Easter, ch. g. 55 by Camelot's Little Cuero 19
1963 Chuckle M Podna, ch. g. 57 by Texas B 11
Glimpse, s. h. 53 by Blackman Burdick 11
1962 Black Lagoon, blk. g. 58 by Alumnus (TB) 9
1961 Sweety Poo, br. h. 56 by Tinky Poo 3½
Tender Boy, s. h. 55 by Bartender 3½
1960 Baldy C, ch. h. 45 by King Clegg 2½
Mescal Brownie, br. g. 55 by Driftwood 2½
Pretty Pokey, dn. h. 48 by Poco Bueno 2½

1959 Joe Lauro, s. h. 50 by Lauro... 2
1958 Melody Mount, bkn. m. 48 by Music Mount.............. 6
1957 Skippity Scoot, pal. h. 52 by Scooter W..................... 9
1956 Squatty, br. g. 51 by Tony L... 5
1955 L M She'll Do, pal. m. 51 by Brush Mount................ 6
1954 Fame Mounty, pal. g. 50 by Cripple Mount.............. 2
1953 Angus Joe, ch. g. 45 by Joe Traveler Jr..................... 2
         Butterscotch Parke, b. m. 48 by General Ike........... 2
         K4 Bisk, ch. g. 49 by Johnny Boy............................. 2
         Shoemaker's Pay Day, b. h. 49 by Nugget McCue S 2
1952 Angus Joe, ch. g. 45 by Joe Traveler Jr..................... 2

WESTERN PLEASURE

1971 Sabrina Lee, b. m. 65 by Jim Harlan...........................460
1970 Pecho Dexter, s. g. 63 by Poco Pecho........................359
1969 Pecho Dexter, s. g. 63 by Poco Pecho........................278
1968 Lady Barbie Sox, s. m. 64 by Double Five..................237½
1967 Pecho Dexter, s. g. 63 by Poco Pecho........................158½
1966 Pecho Dexter, s. g. 63 by Poco Pecho........................145½
1965 Jo Ellen Dun, ch. m. 60 by King's Dun.......................124½
1964 Jo Ellen Dun, ch. m. 60 by King's Dun.......................101
1963 Poco Red Queen, s. m. 60 by Poco Red Ant............. 52
1962 Dell Tommy, br. h. 58 by Poco Dell...........................33½
1961 Dell Tommy, br. h. 58 by Poco Dell...........................31½
1960 Letitia, ch. m. 52 by Texas Tom................................. 23
1959 Mohawk Buck, bkn. g. 50 by Yellow Buck................. 15

TRAIL HORSE

1971 Dell Tommy, br. h. 58 by Poco Dell........................... 61
1970 Little Nebraska, s. g. 58 by Little Sunflower.............. 38
1969 Pecho Dexter, s. g. 63 by Poco Pecho........................ 56
1968 Pecho Dexter, s. g. 63 by Poco Pecho........................ 50
1967 Zora's Lady Jo, gu. m. 61 by Star Sox Jr.................... 39½
1966 Nifty Babydoll, d. m. 63 by Nifty Bee....................... 28½
1965 Nifty Bee, gu. h. 59 by Bee Line............................... 12
1964 Poco Haunt'em, d. g. 60 by Poco Pico....................... 6

JUMPING

1971 Mr. Smoothie, br. g. 65 by Schmacko......................... 54
1970 Mr. Smoothie, br. g. 65 by Schmacko......................... 41
1969 No award
1968 Bob's Bay King, b. g. 60 by Moon King...................... 19
1967 Alfred Riker, br. g. 62 by Loyal Wimpy..................... 33
1966 Alfred Riker, br. g. 62 by Loyal Wimpy..................... 15
1965 King Goaltender, pal. g. 58 by King Star.................... 4

WORKING HUNTER

1971 Mr. Smoothie, br. g. 65 by Schmacko......................... 47
1970 Mr. Smoothie, br. g. 65 by Schmacko......................... 19

1969	Bob's Bay King, b. g. 60 by Moon King	12
1968	Bob's Bay King, b. g. 60 by Moon King	23
1967	Bob's Bay King, b. g. 60 by Moon King	13

ENGLISH PLEASURE

1971	Buckeye 3 Bars, s. h. 65 by Jock Bars	165
1970	Pecho Dexter, s. g. 63 by Poco Pecho	127
1969	Pecho Dexter, s. g. 63 by Poco Pecho	68
1968	Pecho Dexter, s. g. 63 by Poco Pecho	38½

HALTER

1971	Gold Margarita, pal. m. 68 by Mr. Bar Gold	332
1970	Miss Jim 45, d. m. 66 by Jim Harlan	436
1969	Lady Gaines, ch. m. 63 by Aledo Bar	331
1968	Sugar Leda, s. m. 66 by Sugar Bars	379
1967	Roxana Bar, gr. m. 64 by Magnolia Bar	316
1966	Aledolita Bar, s. m. 62 by Aledo Bar	276
1965	Trouble Step, s. m. 64 by Big Step	264
1964	Sonora Sorrell, s. g. 57 by Lauro	198
1963	Aledo Bar's Lady, d. m. 61 by Aledo Bar	178
1962	Poco Margaret, s. m. 58 by Poco Pine	177
1961	Wimpy Leo San, s. h. 59 by Leo San	77
1960	Miss Jazebel, b. m. 58 by Pudden Head	129
1959	Pandarita Hill, ch. m. 54 by Showdown	99
1958	Poco Lynn, dn. m. 54 by Poco Bueno	72
1957	Hank's Sue, ch. m. 53 by Hank H	68
1956	Barbara Star, ch. m. 48 by Star Duster	62
1955	Dee Gee, b. m. 45 by Bartender	69
1954	Pretty Pam, gu. m. 49 by Buckskin Joe	59
1953	Monsieur Joe, br. h. 48 by Red Star Joe	68
1952	Bill Cody, ch. h. 44 by Wimpy	19

• All registered Quarter Horses must be tattoo-branded on the inside of the upper lip with an official identification number, if these horses are to run on official AQHA tracks. The tattoo or number is placed on the horse's registration certificate and becomes part of the identifying papers. This is to prevent the running of "ringers" by dishonest persons. A ringer is a substitute for a less speedy horse. The running of ringers, at both Thoroughbred and Quarter Horse tracks, is impossible when racehorses are tattoo branded.

• More words are written annually about the Quarter Horse than all other equine breeds combined. There are about a dozen magazines devoted exclusively to the breed, and about four dozen magazines and newspapers that regularly publicize the breed.

The chief magazines are those mentioned in Chapter 9, plus the *Western Horseman,* the *Horseman, Eastern Quarter Horse, Quarter Horse of the Pacific Coast, Hoofs and Horns, Quarter and Light Horse Digest,* the *Cattleman, Western Livestock Journal, Horse & Rider, Inter-Mountain Quarter Horse,* the *Ranchman,* and others.

Index